THE K
BOOK OF
CROSSWORDS 2

Dr Gareth Moore is an Ace Puzzler, and author of lots of
puzzle books. He created an online brain-training site
called BrainedUp.com, and runs an online puzzle
site called PuzzleMix.com. Gareth has a PhD from
the University of Cambridge, where he taught
machines to understand spoken English.

Buster Books

First published in Great Britain in 2017 by Buster Books,
an imprint of Michael O'Mara Books Limited,
9 Lion Yard, Tremadoc Road, London SW4 7NQ

 www.mombooks.com/buster   Buster Books   @BusterBooks

Illustrations by John Bigwood

A CIP catalogue record for this book is available from the British Library.

ISBN: 978-1-78055-433-4

5 7 9 10 8 6

Papers used by Buster Books are natural, recyclable products
made from wood grown in sustainable forests. The manufacturing processes
conform to the environmental regulations of the country of origin.

Puzzles designed and typeset by Gareth Moore
www.drgarethmoore.com

Layout designed by Barbara Ward

Printed and bound in March 2019 by CPI Group (UK) Ltd,
108 Beddington Lane, Croydon, CR0 4YY, United Kingdom

Contents

Crossword Crazy!

Crosswords are the most popular printed puzzles of all time. They've been around for over 100 years – so your grandparents probably did them when they were children!

The Rules Of Crosswords

The rules of crosswords are very simple: just find the solution word described by each numbered across or down clue and then write it into the corresponding squares in the grid.

Sometimes, you will be able to think of more than one solution to a clue. When this happens, wait until you solve some of the words that cross over that one in the grid, then use these to help you choose the correct solution.

Each clue has a number in brackets at the end, like this: (4). This shows you how many letters are in the word you are trying to guess and matches the number of empty squares in the grid. Occasionally you might see two numbers, like this: (3, 3). This means there are two words to place, each of the given length, such as 'The End'. Don't leave a space between the words in the grid, though – write one letter in each square.

If you see a ';' in a clue, it means the clue is made up of different parts which will help you guess the solution. For example, the clue: 'Opposite of front; rear of your body (4)' provides two clues for 'back'.

The puzzles in this book are divided in to four different sizes, getting harder as you work through the book.

If you get stuck and simply can't find a word and fear you will go crazy, don't despair, all the answers are in the back

There's a 'Time' line at the top of every page for you to write in how long it took you to do each puzzle.

Good luck, and have fun! There's a 'Time' line at the top of every page for you to write in how long it took you to do each puzzle.

Good luck, and have fun!

Level One:
Beginners

Puzzle 1

Across
1 You see the world with these (4)
4 A rotation between two lines, measured in degrees (5)
5 Cry about something really sad (4)

Down
1 Formal school test (4)
2 Large bird that is a symbol of the USA (5)
3 The opposite of shallow (4)

Puzzle 2

Across
3 Fame; honour (5)
5 Have a need to pay something back (3)
6 A mix of cold, raw vegetables served as a meal (5)

Down
1 Large cape, like a cartoon villain might wear (5)
2 Food that's bought in loaves (5)
4 Hooting, night-time bird of prey (3)

Puzzle 3

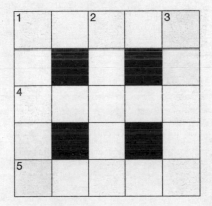

Across
1 Come into flower (5)
4 Lazy start to the day (3-2)
5 Food product made by bees (5)

Down
1 Burp (5)
2 Large sea (5)
3 Coins or notes used to buy things (5)

Puzzle 4

Across

1 Male deer (4)
4 Cereal plant used to make flour (5)
5 The reflection of a sound, so you hear it again (4)

Down

2 You bite your food with these (5)
3 Fetch; obtain (3)
4 Sorrow; misfortune (3)

Puzzle 5

Across
1 Direction in which the sun sets (4)
3 Film seen at the cinema (5)
4 Underwear worn on your top half to keep you warm (4)

Down
1 Still in one piece (5)
2 Extremely holy person (5)

Puzzle 6

Across
1 Say words (5)
4 Grumble (5)
5 Animal kept for wool and meat (5)

Down
2 Place where a bird sits (5)
3 Really surprise (5)

Puzzle 7

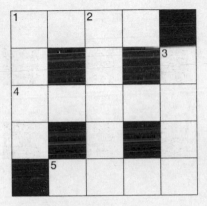

Across

1 Clean with water (4)
4 Large area of land for growing crops (5)
5 Notice; see (4)

Down

1 Woman married to a husband (4)
2 Clean the floor with a broom (5)
3 Make changes to something that's been written (4)

Puzzle 8

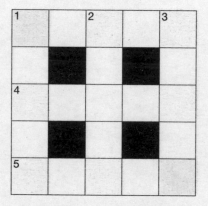

Across
1 A square, triangle or pentagon, for example (5)
4 Book of maps (5)
5 You dry your face or hands with this (5)

Down
1 A word shouted at the beginning of a race (5)
2 Let someone do something; permit (5)
3 A stand used by an artist while painting (5)

Puzzle 9

Across

3 Absolutely necessary (5)
5 Father (3)
6 Magical being that can
   grant wishes (5)

Down

1 Someone travelling on
   a horse (5)
2 Device that can pick up
   music transmissions from
   the air (5)
4 You get this from exposing
   your skin to the sun (3)

Puzzle 10

Across

1 Choose from a selection of items (4)
3 Country whose capital is Tokyo (5)
4 Make another identical version of something (4)

Down

1 Musical instrument with lots of black and white keys (5)
2 Mad; nutty (5)

Puzzle 11

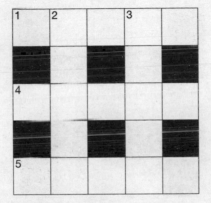

Across

1 Common type of cat with dark stripes (5)
4 Faithful; trusty (5)
5 Prepared to do something (5)

Down

2 On your own; by yourself (5)
3 Hair that hangs from a man's chin and cheeks (5)

Puzzle 12

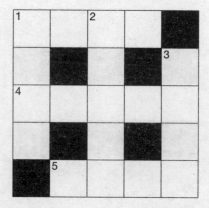

Across

1 Close your teeth on something (4)
4 Indian sauce-based food that's often spicy (5)
5 Outer covering for your foot (4)

Down

1 The part of your body that's behind you (4)
2 Portable light (5)
3 Write using a keyboard (4)

Puzzle 13

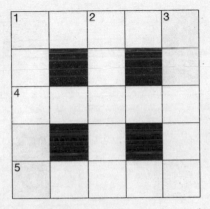

Across

1 Land that borders the sea (5)
4 More of something, as in "I want ___ ketchup" (5)
5 Compass point that's often "up" on a map (5)

Down

1 Wash and remove dirt and stains (5)
2 A person performing in a play (5)
3 Give a lesson at school (5)

Puzzle 14

Across
1 Hut for storing gardening tools (4)
4 The crime of stealing (5)
5 Something you drive a car along (4)

Down
2 Wild, wolf-like animal famous for its laugh (5)
3 A small round mark or spot (3)
4 A thick, black liquid used for surfacing streets (3)

Time ....

Puzzle 15

Across
1 Large bag carried by Father Christmas (4)
3 White powder used when making bread or cakes (5)
4 Small amphibian, found in garden ponds (4)

Down
1 Work out a solution (5)
2 The edge of a piece of bread (5)

Puzzle 16

Across
1 Woody shoot on a tree branch (4)
4 People who don't tell the truth (5)
5 Lovingly touch someone with your lips (4)

Down
2 Kitchen item used for beating eggs or cream (5)
3 Female children; not boys but ___ (5)

Puzzle 17

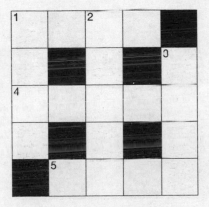

Across
1. Piece of string used to tie up a shoe (4)
4. Move on hands and knees (5)
5. A small island (4)

Down
1. Device for stopping someone from opening a door (4)
2. Group of children all taught together (5)
3. Substance used for sticking things together (4)

 **BEGINNERS** **Time** ....

Puzzle 18

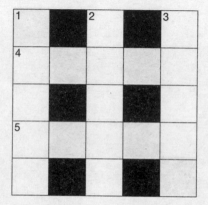

Across

4 Animal used for pulling carriages (5)

5 Small boat that you move with a paddle (5)

Down

1 Of a significant width or depth, like a really long book (5)

2 Not right, like a question that has is incorrect (5)

3 Precious stone, like you might find in a ring (5)

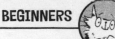
Puzzle 19

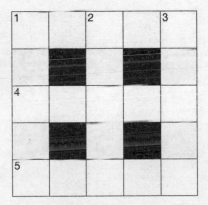

Across

1 Invisible creature that is said to haunt a place (5)
4 Go into a room (5)
5 Sight, hearing, touch, taste or smell (5)

Down

1 An answer you give but which you don't know to be correct (5)
2 Many times; frequently (5)
3 The number of corners on a triangle (5)

Puzzle 20

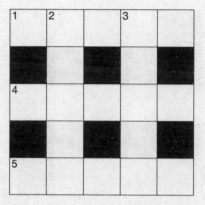

Across
1 A sphere with a map of the world on it (5)
4 Something special that you really enjoy (5)
5 How far down something goes, like water in a swimming pool (5)

Down
2 Big; of a greater size than average (5)
3 Tell everyone how amazing you are (5)

Puzzle 21

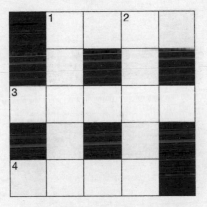

Across

1 This as well; too (4)
3 A house built from blocks of snow (5)
4 Cover something in paper, such as a present (4)

Down

1 If you lose your temper you might feel this emotion (5)
2 Type of spoon used for serving ice cream (5)

 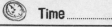

Puzzle 22

Across

1 Short version of "Christmas" (4)

4 Make a change to something (5)

5 A thing that needs to be done (4)

Down

2 School subject involving numbers (5)

3 What you might call a male teacher (3)

4 Appropriate; suitable (3)

Puzzle 23

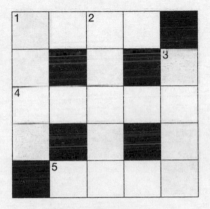

Across
1 Superhero's jacket (4)
4 What you might be after spinning around in circles (5)
5 A solemn promise, like when someone swears on the bible (4)

Down
1 A system for writing a secret message (4)
2 Baked dough covered with cheese, tomato and other toppings (5)
3 Traditional story about gods and heroes (4)

Puzzle 24

Across

1 A narrow road for walking along (4)
4 Small, winged creature with magic powers, like Tinkerbell (5)
5 A printed set of restaurant meal options (4)

Down

2 Something you might set to wake you up in the morning (5)
3 A wading bird with long thin legs (5)

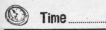

Puzzle 25

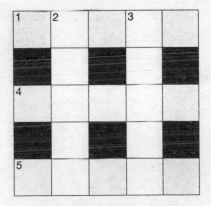

Across

1 The opposite of light, in terms of weight (5)
4 Green plant that makes up a lawn (5)
5 Statement that is honest and accurate (5)

Down

2 A fault with a computer program (5)
3 A brief trip to a location (5)

Puzzle 26

Across

3 Someone taught by a teacher (5)
5 Instinctive thought: a ___ feeling (3)
6 A piece of furniture with legs and a flat top (5)

Down

1 This is often added to drinks to make them sweeter (5)
2 The name of a book (5)
4 Tavern; public house (3)

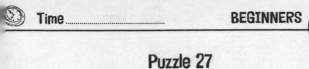

Puzzle 27

Across

1 Small medical tablet that must be swallowed (4)

3 Something that you are unsure about (5)

4 Aluminium sheet that's used to wrap food (4)

Down

1 A picture taken with a camera (5)

2 Something attached to an item to say who owns it (5)

Puzzle 28

Across
1 A long way away (4)
4 Female fox (5)
5 Walk through shallow water (4)

Down
2 Repaired (5)
3 Took part in a sprint race (3)
4 Solemn promise (3)

Puzzle 29

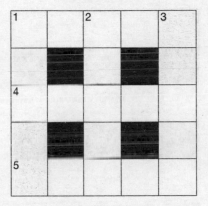

Across

1 A trench used to carry water (5)
4 The time of day when it's dark (5)
5 A lesson to take away from a story (5)

Down

1 Cloth used to make jeans (5)
2 A striped yellow and black big cat, found in Asia (5)
3 Type of building you might stay in on holiday (5)

Puzzle 30

Across
1 Common; ordinary (5)
4 The result of adding up some numbers (5)
5 Vegetables that might be baked, green or broad (5)

Down
2 Loud breathing noise made during sleep (5)
3 One more time (5)

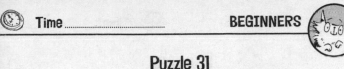
Puzzle 31

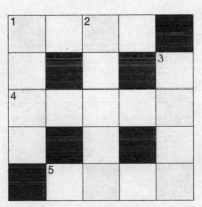

Across
1 Small restaurant (4)
4 Sound made by a sheep or goat (5)
5 Fried potato product (4)

Down
1 Six-sided solid which has all faces of equal size (4)
2 Recently made; not tinned, frozen or preserved (5)
3 Movement of one leg in front of the other while walking (4)

Puzzle 32

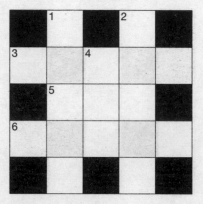

Across

3 A special playing card that isn't part of the regular pack of 52 cards (5)

5 Clever humour; a funny person (3)

6 A prize given for bravery, or for winning something (5)

Down

1 A tall building, such as a skyscraper (5)

2 A single segment of a flower (5)

4 Small child (3)

Puzzle 33

Across

1 What a red light on a traffic signal tells you to do (4)
4 A detailed plan or map (5)
5 Common edible fish, often served in sandwiches or a salad (4)

Down

2 Vehicle that pulls carriages along rails (5)
3 A light touch of the hand (3)
4 A baby's bed (3)

Puzzle 34

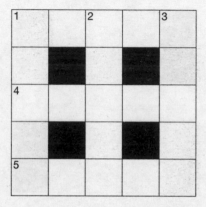

Across
1 A book for keeping a day-by-day record of what happened (5)
4 A room at the top of a house, above the top level (5)
5 The gold medal position in a race (5)

Down
1 One of Snow White's helpers (5)
2 The central table in a church, where the priest stands (5)
3 A sailing boat (5)

Puzzle 35

Across
1 Get bigger as time passes (4)
4 Go up a ladder (5)
5 Soft beaches are covered in this (4)

Down
2 The instructions for a competition or event (5)
3 A lady, as opposed to a man (5)

Puzzle 36

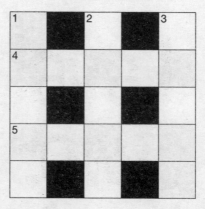

Across

4 Plenty; more than enough (5)

5 A strong feeling of fear where you don't know what to do (5)

Down

1 What you usually are when you are smiling (5)

2 Use money to buy something (5)

3 Sandy seashore (5)

Level Two:
Intermediates

Puzzle 37

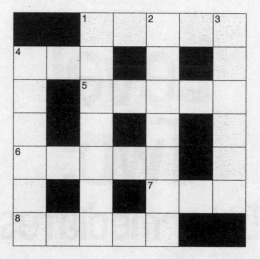

Across
1 A fright (5)
4 The highest part of something (3)
5 Message sent from one computer to another (5)
6 Without any clothes on (5)
7 Paddle used to row a boat (3)
8 Alarm on an ambulance or police car (5)

Down
1 Person who is talking (7)
2 Leave behind (7)
3 Long cake filled with cream and covered with chocolate (6)
4 Sport played at Wimbledon (6)

Puzzle 38

Across
3 A bicycle seat (6)
4 Take part in a play (3)
5 Something you say when you meet someone (5)
7 A word used to refer to one or more of something, as in "___ quantity" (3)
8 Do not permit (6)

Down
1 A casual word for a close friend (4)
2 A nut that is marzipan is made from (6)
3 Place where children go to be taught (6)
6 Wild animal's home (4)

Puzzle 39

Across

1 Young sheep (4)
5 Type of woodwind instrument (4)
7 Group of singers (5)
9 Purchase an item (3)
10 Did light, as in "I ___ the candle" (3)
11 Not very big (5)
13 Cause to go to a particular destination, like mail (4)
14 Create a picture on a piece of paper (4)

Down

2 Charged with a crime, as in "he ___ the man of stealing" (7)
3 Something a ghost might shout (3)
4 Powerful ape found in central Africa (7)
6 Restaurants give you this at the end of a meal (4)
8 Religious song (4)
12 Total two numbers together (3)

Puzzle 40

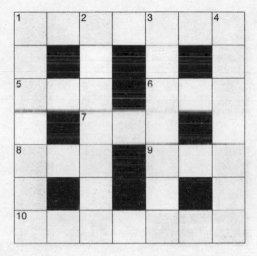

Across

1 Ghost (7)
5 Chew food and swallow (3)
6 People who play music at discos (abbr) (3)
7 Long, thin stick (3)
8 Biblical couple, Adam and ___ (3)
9 Say something that isn't true (3)
10 Completely ruin (7)

Down

1 Imagine something that isn't real (7)
2 A woman who plays a part in a play (7)
3 A small fish, like you might see in a stream (7)
4 Something strange or unexplained (7)

Puzzle 41

Across

2 A round flat dish that a meal is served on (5)

4 Hot-tasting yellow food paste, sometimes added to ham (7)

5 The other side, in a battle (5)

Down

1 Large, black leopard (7)

2 Hold a video on its current picture (5)

3 What you are if you arrive before the start of an event (5)

Puzzle 42

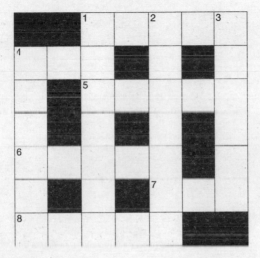

Across

1 Trousers made of denim (5)
4 Which person? (3)
5 Beneath (5)
6 Move in time to music (5)
7 Droop to a lower level (3)
8 The vertical sides of a
  room (5)

Down

1 Personal diary (7)
2 Details of where someone
  lives (7)
3 Thin rope used for tying
  things (6)
4 Opening in a wall, usually
  filled with glass (6)

Puzzle 43

Across

1 Spaghetti, lasagne or ravioli, for example (5)
4 Something a man might wear with a shirt (3)
6 Our planet (5)
7 Theatre show with sung music (5)
8 "The person to whom I am talking" (3)
9 The rate at which something is moving (5)

Down

1 Attractive (6)
2 Solemn; thoughtful (7)
3 Sports player (7)
5 Short journey to deliver or fetch something for someone else (6)

Puzzle 44

Across

3 Something you might carry water in on a beach (6)

4 Evergreen tree with needle-like leaves (3)

5 Large, white waterbird (5)

7 Owns; possesses (3)

8 Erasable writing tool (6)

Down

1 Currency used in many European countries (4)

2 Breakfast food served in a bowl (6)

3 Larger (6)

6 Boat for travelling at sea (4)

Puzzle 45

Across
1 Small creature that helps Santa (3)
3 Metal container (3)
5 Opposite of high (3)
6 Barnyard sound (3)
7 Sick; not well (3)
8 You can travel quickly down a snowy slope by using two of these (3)
9 A sharp pull on something (3)
11 Use your eyes (3)

12 A small part of something (3)
13 Tear something, such as a piece of paper (3)

Down
1 Tall tree with broad leaves (3)
2 Someone who sells flowers (7)
3 Bird chirp sound (7)
4 Nothing; zero (3)
8 Cry uncontrollably (3)
10 A space between two things (3)

Puzzle 46

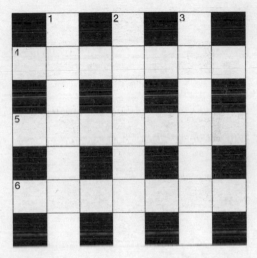

Across
4 Bedclothes (7)
5 Key hot dog ingredient (7)
6 An Italian meal made from rice (7)

Down
1 Large, triangular Egyptian monument (7)
2 Very big, grand house (7)
3 Badly behaved (7)

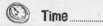

Puzzle 47

Across

1 Vegetable used to make chips (6)
4 Vertical row in a table (6)
5 A purple colour found in the rainbow (6)
6 Hidden; not told to others (6)

Down

1 Pledge that you will do something (7)
2 Loud noise heard during a storm (7)
3 This evening (7)

Puzzle 48

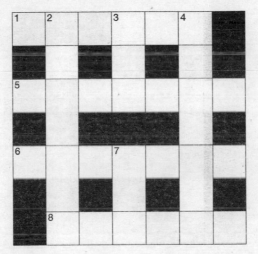

Across

1 Not very wide (6)
5 A sad theatre play (7)
6 Nose opening (7)
8 Box for animals to eat from (6)

Down

2 Place where planes take off and land (7)
3 Old scrap of cloth (3)
4 Marriage ceremony (7)
7 A pair (3)

Puzzle 49

Across

1 Creature often mistaken for a frog (4)
3 More than one but less than several (3)
5 The Queen's favourite dog (5)
6 Christmas song (5)
7 Hot drink, often brewed from a bag (3)
8 You wear shoes on these (4)

Down

1 Piece of paper used for admission (6)
2 The second largest continent (6)
3 Savage and aggressive (6)
4 Carry case for money and cards (6)

Puzzle 50

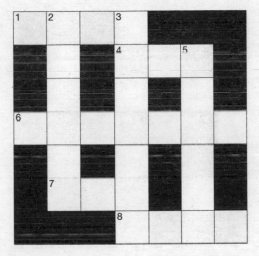

Across

1 Jump into the air (4)
4 The blackened remains of a fire (3)
6 Two-wheeled vehicle with a saddle (7)
7 Large, ostrich-like bird (3)
8 Maths problems (4)

Down

2 Group of countries under one ruler (6)
3 Ancient Egyptian paper (7)
5 Gas sometimes used to fill balloons (6)

Puzzle 51

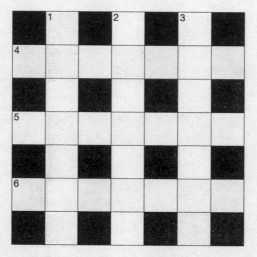

Across
4 Not very common (7)
5 Itch yourself (7)
6 Wheeled shopping cart (7)

Down
1 Make-believe, one-horned animal (7)
2 Someone who lives in Israel (7)
3 Bag for school books (7)

Puzzle 52

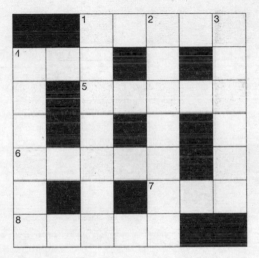

Across

1 What this book is printed on (5)
4 Illness often caught in the winter (3)
5 An item of clothing worn by women (5)
6 The opposite of black (5)
7 Brazil, hazel or almond, for example (3)
8 The opposite direction to left (5)

Down

1 Sweet dessert (7)
2 You might receive this at Christmas (7)
3 The outcome of something, such as a test (6)
4 Colourful plant (6)

Puzzle 53

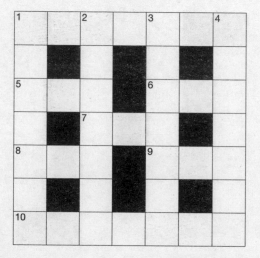

Across

1 Narrow strips of pasta (7)
5 You might wipe your feet on this when entering a building (3)
6 Abbreviation for the day after Wednesday (3)
7 Not at home (3)
8 Tidal movement away from the land (3)

9 Operate, as in "I will ___ the computer" (3)
10 A large snake (7)

Down

1 One, two and three are ___ (7)
2 Halloween month (7)
3 Green, leafy salad vegetable (7)
4 Someone who studies at university (7)

Puzzle 54

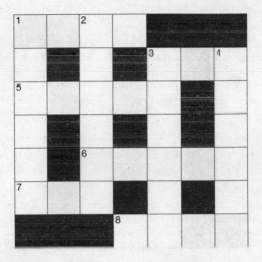

Across
1 Stopped living (4)
3 Implement used for cleaning floors (3)
5 Powder used for making chocolate drinks (5)
6 Tall playground ride (5)
7 Fish eggs (3)
8 Warm up (4)

Down
1 Person who looks after the sick (6)
2 Something you give to try and avoid blame (6)
3 A word that means "found in the sea" (6)
4 Mother or father (6)

Puzzle 55

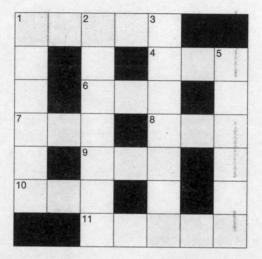

Across

1 Tasting like sugar (5)
4 Choose something (3)
6 Round, green vegetable that grows in a pod (3)
7 Female sheep (3)
8 The male equivalent of "daughter" (3)
9 Large rodent that once spread the plague (3)
10 Also; as well (3)
11 In the countryside, away from town (5)

Down

1 Public road (6)
2 The ruler of an empire (7)
3 Device for grilling bread (7)
5 Underground passage (6)

Puzzle 56

Across

3 Travel behind someone (6)
4 The whole quantity of something (3)
5 Not yet old (5)
7 Snake-shaped fish (3)
8 Pass on an illness to another person (6)

Down

1 Part of a song sung by just one person (4)
2 Fail to remember (6)
3 Travelling through the air, like a bird (6)
6 The body part that connects your head to your body (4)

Puzzle 57

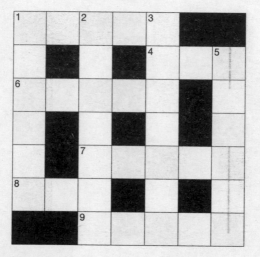

Across
1 A prize given for an achievement (5)
4 Mischievous child (3)
6 Where a pop concert might take place (5)
7 Elephants' tusks are made of this (5)
8 Abbreviation for a sixtieth of a minute (3)
9 Small, poisonous snake (5)

Down
1 Counting tool with sliding beads (6)
2 The United States (7)
3 A precious jewel often used to decorate rings (7)
5 Solemn request to God (6)

Puzzle 58

Across

2 What a piece of wood usually does on water (5)

4 Decayed grass and plant material, used to help other plants grow (7)

5 Cutlery companion to a fork (5)

Down

1 Friendly sea animal with a fin (7)

2 A group of sheep (5)

3 Flavour (5)

Puzzle 59

Across

1 Jelly-like substance (3)
3 Speak out loud (3)
5 Elderly person (inits) (3)
6 Gang or crowd who are hard to control (3)
7 What comes out of a pen (3)
8 A word to specify the opposite of something, as in "I will do this but ___ that" (3)
9 If you cut yourself, you may need first ___ (3)
11 Abbreviation that means "and so on" (3)

12 An armed conflict between two or more countries (3)
13 Dry grass, used as food for animals (3)

Down

1 The pink flesh around your teeth (3)
2 Red, edible shellfish with two big claws (7)
3 Dark green, leafy vegetable (7)
4 Long-haired ox, found in Tibet (3)
8 At once (3)
10 Home decorating (inits) (3)

Puzzle 60

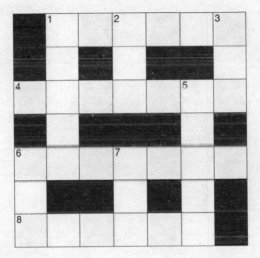

Across

1 The opposite of private (6)
4 Activity where you sing along with words on a screen (7)
6 Waterproof boots (7)
8 A shape or sign that represents a particular meaning (6)

Down

1 Quiet time without noise (5)
2 Sheep's bleat (3)
3 Stick used to play pool or snooker (3)
5 What you do when you get down on your knees (5)
6 Used to be (3)
7 Scientist's workplace (3)

Puzzle 61

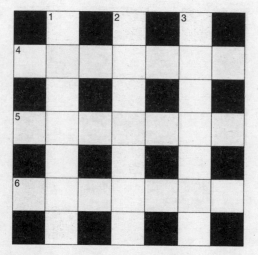

Across

4 Lightweight waterproof coat (7)
5 The gathering of crops (7)
6 Someone who educates you (7)

Down

1 Soft toffee (7)
2 Criminal who has been found guilty (7)
3 Spectacles (7)

Puzzle 62

Across

3 Trip to see wild animals in their natural homes (6)
4 Substance used for making crayons and candles (3)
5 What the Sun provides for us (5)
7 What we breathe (3)
8 Picture made with small, coloured tiles (6)

Down

1 A car with a driver who you pay to take you somewhere (4)
2 The area around the NorthPole (6)
3 Large, edible fish with pink flesh (6)
6 The thread-like strands that grow on your head (4)

Puzzle 63

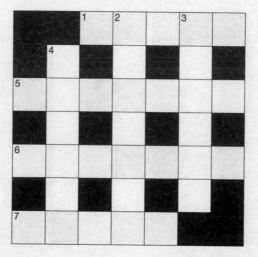

Across

1 The sky beyond the atmosphere (5)
5 Toy with two wheels, which you stand on and power by foot (7)
6 Let go; set free (7)
7 Without any contents (5)

Down

2 A series of related tasks for an overall goal (7)
3 Cheddar, brie or stilton, for example (6)
4 What you might do if you saw a ghost (6)

Puzzle 64

Across
2 What you do at night (5)
4 Gets hotter (5,2)
5 Loud, non-musical sound (5)

Down
1 Mythical creature with a woman's body and a fish's tail (7)
2 If you spill ink, you might leave a ___ (5)
3 Dried plum, eaten as a snack (5)

Puzzle 65

Across

1 Strip of material worn around the neck to keep you warm (5)
4 A type of cereal, sometimes used in bread and biscuits (3)
6 Abbreviation for the day after Monday (3)
7 It might be sunflower or olive, and is used in cooking (3)
8 What you might serve tea in (3)
9 Large-horned deer (3)
10 You need this to hear anything (3)
11 Piece of paper (5)

Down

1 To move your hand gently over something, like a cat or dog (6)
2 A deer's horns (7)
3 Small, brown mark on the skin (7)
5 Someone who knows a lot about a subject (6)

Puzzle 66

Across
1 A heavy disc thrown during athletic events (6)
5 Colourful plants (7)
6 Large seabird with a big pouch in its beak for holding fish (7)
8 The time when the sun goes below the horizon (6)

Down
2 Sickness (7)
3 Farmyard animal that produces most of the milk we drink (3)
4 A person's last name (7)
7 A small hotel (3)

Puzzle 67

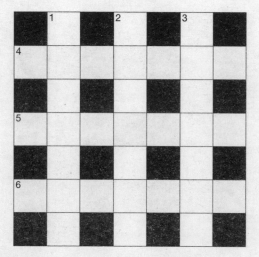

Across

4 Line where the sky meets the Earth (7)

5 Shake with fear (7)

6 Person being treated by a doctor (7)

Down

1 Small outdoor carpet for wiping your feet on (7)

2 Post sent around the world by aeroplane (7)

3 Young goose (7)

Puzzle 68

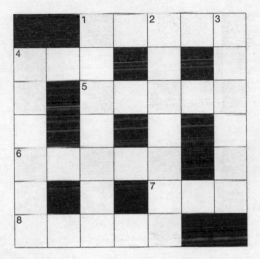

Across

1 Something a witch might cast (5)
4 There are five at the end of your foot (3)
5 Turns over and over (5)
6 You stick this on a letter before you post it (5)
7 Male child (3)
8 A unit used to measure quantities of liquid (5)

Down

1 A person who performs household duties for others (7)
2 Event where the Moon moves in front of the Sun (7)
3 Teaching session at school (6)
4 Glittery material used to decorate Christmas trees (6)

Puzzle 69

Across

1 A set of two things (4)
4 A bird might lay this (3)
6 First month of the year (7)
7 Substance used to colour hair or clothes (3)
8 Selection of food to help someone become healthier (4)

Down

2 On a ship or plane (6)
3 Decreased (7)
5 Building to park a car in (6)

Puzzle 70

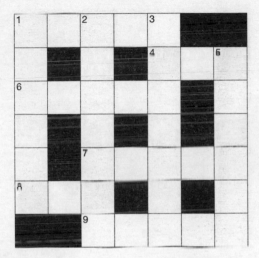

Across

1 To hurl an object, perhaps to another person (5)
4 Limb connected to your shoulder (3)
6 It's used for drawing straight lines (5)
7 Two times (5)
8 The part of your body used to see (3)
9 Unclean (5)

Down

1 Sea animal with a hard shell on its back (6)
2 People belonging to the same family are ___ (7)
3 A person famous for fighting in battle (7)
5 Great unhappiness (6)

Puzzle 71

Across
1 You might look in this to see yourself (6)
4 A maths puzzle, perhaps (7)
6 Ancient Egyptian king (7)
8 Two times ten (6)

Down
1 Third month of the year (5)
2 Steal something (3)
3 Male sheep (3)
5 Hard black wood, sometimes used for piano keys (5)
6 Container for flowers (3)
7 Move quickly on foot (3)

Puzzle 72

Across
1 A period of one hundred years (7)
5 Absolute quiet (7)
6 Slow-moving mass of ice (7)

Down
1 Car, boat or aeroplane, for example (7)
2 Pull something so as to make it longer (7)
3 Thin, crispy biscuit (7)

Puzzle 73

Across

3 Water or oil, for example (6)
4 Plead for something (3)
5 Heavenly messenger (5)
7 Stopping at en route, as in "The train went from London to Manchester ___ Birmingham" (3)
8 Unwanted animals that cause problems (6)

Down

1 Road marker which shows which way to go (4)
2 Stringed instrument played with a bow (6)
3 Someone in charge of a group (6)
6 Incredibly wicked (4)

Puzzle 74

Across

1 Small stone that you find on a beach (6)
5 Bird that you might find at a stately home (7)
6 Something that women often carry with them (7)
8 A discussion involving different points of view (6)

Down

2 The colour of the city in "The Wizard of Oz" (7)
3 Channel that's usually number 1 on a TV (inits) (3)
4 Put a magic spell on someone (7)
7 Touch gently with a tissue, perhaps to clean or dry (3)

Puzzle 75

Across

1 A black, noisy bird (4)
4 That man or boy's (3)
6 Final course of a meal (7)
7 Female equivalent of "he" (3)
8 Great anger (4)

Down

2 Becomes ready to eat, as fruit (6)
3 Speak softly (7)
5 Opposite of weak (6)

Puzzle 76

Across

1 Not very happy (5)
5 From Great Britain (7)
6 Sports umpire (7)
7 Wound caused by a bee or wasp (5)

Down

2 Repeated visual design (7)
3 Christian festival during spring (6)
4 Religious leader (6)

Puzzle 77

Across

1 Clever (5)
4 Tell a fib (3)
5 An item worn over the front of the body to protect clothes (5)
6 You have one on each hand (5)
7 Playing card "1" (3)
8 Someone who flies an aeroplane (5)

Down

1 Common white or grey seabird (7)
2 Circus entertainer who leaps around (7)
3 You use this whenever you lick something (6)
4 Portable computer (6)

Puzzle 78

Across

1 Happy to live with humans, if an animal (4)
3 Red area directly above or below the mouth (3)
5 Cowboy contest (5)
6 Midday meal (5)
7 Female deer (3)
8 Selfish; not generous (4)

Down

1 Long piece of cotton used for sewing (6)
2 Mix up (6)
3 Sitting room (6)
4 Large snake that kills prey by crushing them (6)

Puzzle 79

Across

1 Rough drawing (6)
4 The season when leaves fall from the trees (6)
5 Male parent (6)
6 Fuel used in many cars (6)

Down

1 Mix up a deck of playing cards ready for a game (7)
2 Imaginary ring around the middle of the Earth (7)
3 Hide (7)

Puzzle 80

Across
1 In a state of slumber (6)
5 Soldiers on horseback (7)
6 Write a piece of music (7)
8 Hang or swing loosely (6)

Down
2 Edible fish or shellfish (7)
3 A long period of history (3)
4 Sun umbrella used to provide shade (7)
7 Metal fastening you might use to attach paper to a board (3)

Puzzle 81

Across
1 Young dog (5)
5 Common ice-cream flavour (7)
6 Absolutely dedicated (7)
7 Stomach (5)

Down
2 Fixed set of clothes to be worn to school (7)
3 Powder inside a flower that bees collect (6)
4 Rich, moist cake (6)

Puzzle 82

Across

3 A message sent by post (6)
4 Very large expanse of water (3)
5 Fruit used for making wine (5)
7 Large water vessel, like you might serve tea in a cafeteria from (3)
8 Something said to cause offence (6)

Down

1 Fruit related to the apple, wider at the base than at the top (4)
2 Large area of dry land, often covered in sand (6)
3 A very old story that is claimed to be true (6)
6 Tug down on something (4)

Puzzle 83

Across
1 Sleeveless cloak (4)
3 Centre of a wheel (3)
5 Doctor's assistant (5)
6 Bitter, yellow fruit (5)
7 Wonder (3)
8 Scratch (4)

Down
1 Somewhere you might go to see a film (6)
2 Colour made by mixing red and blue (6)
3 Hard hat used to protect the head (6)
4 Tree limb (6)

Puzzle 84

Across
1 Thought (4)
4 Louse sometimes found in hair (3)
6 Brave; courageous (7)
7 Heavy unit of weight (3)
8 Unit measured in seconds (4)

Down
2 Leave; go away from (6)
3 Extremely old (7)
5 Bicycle for two people (6)

Puzzle 85

Across

1 Vision (5)
4 Having lived for a long time (3)
6 Deity; a being that is worshipped (3)
7 Thick floor mat (3)
8 Wild animal's home (3)
9 What you might write in a chat message to indicate laughing (inits) (3)
10 Shade of colour (3)
11 A word you say to apologise (5)

Down

1 Look for something (6)
2 Eye coverings worn for swimming (7)
3 Young child who has just started to walk (7)
5 Horse-like animal with long ears (6)

Puzzle 86

Across

1 Tell someone you think the same thing (5)
5 Trip away from home for a break (7)
6 Small bird of prey (7)
7 A made-up tale (5)

Down

2 Shiny powder used in crafts to make things sparkle (7)
3 What the white surface of teeth is made of (6)
4 Trustworthy (6)

Puzzle 87

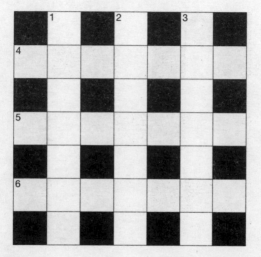

Across
4 Rotate, like a turntable (7)
5 Young tree that's just been planted (7)
6 Type of mountain that erupts with molten lava (7)

Down
1 Six-sided shape (7)
2 Try to form a set of things, such as stamps or stickers (7)
3 The time of day when the sun sets (7)

Puzzle 88

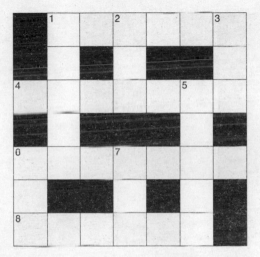

Across

1 Season between spring and winter (6)
4 Unfreeze (7)
6 Loud brass instrument (7)
8 Crayon-like colouring stick (6)

Down

1 Make a serious promise (5)
2 Spoil; make something less good (3)
3 Deep groove made by wheels (3)
5 Take without permission (5)
6 Something that controls the flow of water (3)
7 Joined someone at an agreed place (3)

Puzzle 89

Across

3 Of enormous size, like the universe (6)
4 If I like someone, I might say "I like ___" (3)
5 What a blue light on an ambulance might do (5)
7 "Look over here!" (3)
8 The opposite of "junior" (6)

Down

1 Illegal move in a sport (4)
2 Further up in the air (6)
3 Type of drink found in a cappucino (6)
6 A place where things can be bought (4)

Puzzle 90

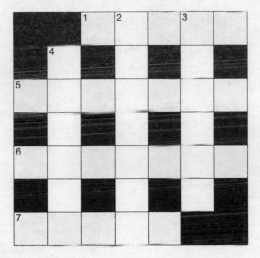

Across

1 Tool used for digging (5)
5 Tomato sauce (7)
6 Thick, sticky liquid made from sugar (7)
7 High body temperature (5)

Down

2 Parcel or bundle (7)
3 Twice (6)
4 Unit used for measuring angles (6)

Puzzle 91

Across
2 Something you sit in (5)
4 Flowers growing on a fruit tree (7)
5 Sets out on a yacht (5)

Down
1 Long and thin yellow root vegetable (7)
2 Phones someone up (5)
3 Underground parts of a tree (5)

Puzzle 92

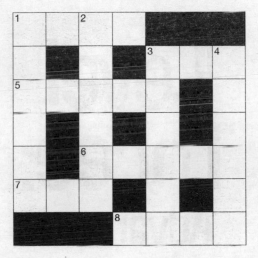

Across

1 Good thing that happens by chance (4)
3 Go bad; decay (3)
5 Raised platform for theatre shows (5)
6 Of exactly the same value (5)
7 And not, as in "neither this ___ that" (3)
8 Tiny biting fly (4)

Down

1 Use your ears (6)
2 The mouth of a volcano (6)
3 Go back (6)
4 Place you go when you need to relieve yourself (6)

Level Three: Advanced

Puzzle 93

Across

1 Hard sweet on a stick (8)
5 Make a hole in the ground with a spade (3)
6 Joint connecting your leg to your foot (5)
8 Moving staircase (9)
10 Flower used for making chains (5)
13 Overhead shot in tennis (3)
15 Opposite of exit (8)

Down

1 Boy (3)
2 Smart thinking (5)
3 Writing device (3)
4 Friend (3)
6 Narrow street or passage (5)
7 Do something wrong (3)
8 The point where something stops (3)
9 Bird's claw (5)
11 Tool used for chopping wood (3)
12 Rest on a chair (3)
14 Word said to someone when you leave (3)

Across

1 Hard covering over a healing cut or graze (4)
4 Not at home (4)
7 Place with houses, shops, offices and buildings (4)
8 Sleep lightly; nap (4)
9 Instrument often used to play jazz (9)
12 Back (4)
14 When you breathe in, you fill this with air (4)
16 Shout loudly (4)
17 Long, deep breath when you are tired (4)

Down

1 Took a seat (3)
2 Long-necked musical instrument with strings to pluck (5)
3 Unhappy (3)
5 Round spinning toy (2-2)
6 At this place (4)
9 Painful (4)
10 Photograph taken of the inside of the body (1-3)
11 Berried plant associated with Christmas (5)
13 Colour of blood (3)
15 Weapon that fires bullets (3)

Across

5 Rub out (5)
6 Went for a fast jog (3)
7 Flash during a thunderstorm (9)
8 Bird found in a pear tree in a Christmas song (9)
11 Expert (abbr) (3)
12 On a computer you ___ a button to make something happen (5)

Down

1 Fruit or vegetable skin (4)
2 Australian animal that moves by jumping (8)
3 Written words (4)
4 Warm and comfortable (4)
6 Animals that pull Santa's sleigh (8)
8 Head of the Roman Catholic Church (4)
9 Key requirement for a tug-of-war (4)
10 Very simple (4)

Across

4 Set of people (5)
6 Narrow (4)
7 Up until now, as in "I haven't told anyone ___" (3)
9 First half of the day (7)
10 Place where wild animals are kept for people to see (3)
12 Coloured part of the eye (4)
13 Vegetable that makes you cry (5)

Down

1 Pay no attention to (6)
2 Figure of a person burned on Bonfire Night (3)
3 Soap for washing your hair (7)
5 Bird associated with the South Pole (7)
8 Sea raider who came to Britain a thousand years ago (6)
11 A single item (3)

Across

1 Triangular Indian snack (6)
4 Question someone (3)
5 Conversation (4)
7 Small bang (3)
10 Very bad (5)
11 Auction item (3)
13 Herb often used to season lamb (4)
16 The atmosphere all around us (3)
17 Angry mood (6)

Down

1 The space above the earth (3)
2 Waterproof coat (3)
3 Painter (6)
4 In the past (3)
6 Large mound (4)
7 On time; without delay (6)
8 Unpleasant feeling caused by injury (4)
9 Gone bad, like fruit (3)
12 Your and my (3)
14 Money you might give to a waiter after a meal (3)
15 Common road vehicle (3)

ADVANCED

Time

Across

1 Animal that might be Persian or tabby (3)
3 Big piece of bread (4)
5 Pastry dish filled with meat or fruit (3)
6 Cut the grass (3)
8 The sound that goes with video (5)
9 Greasy substance cut off meat, such as the rind on bacon (3)
10 Repeatedly bother or scold someone (3)
11 Streets (5)
13 Stop living (3
15 Something a child plays with (3)
17 Green "Star Wars" Jedi master, he is (4)

18 Uncooked (3)

Down

1 Soft, flat hat (3)
2 Building where plays are performed (7)
3 Noisy; not quiet (4)
4 To and ___; going backwards and forwards (3)
6 Frightening creature (7)
7 False hair worn on the head (3)
9 Ate (3)
12 A measurement that's equal to the width times the length (4)
14 Slippery with the cold (3)
16 Evergreen tree with red berries (3)

Across

1 The sound a snake makes (4)
4 Far up in the air (4)
7 A group of three people (4)
8 The direction from which the Sun rises (4)
9 Colourful winged insect (9)
12 The hard part at the end of your finger (4)
14 Not pleasant to look at (4)
16 The world's second-largest cat, after the tiger (4)
17 Slightly wet (4)

Down

1 Very warm (3)
2 Not very tall (5)
3 Grow old (3)
5 Fraction sometimes written as 1/2 (4)
6 Remain in the same place (4)
9 Company who looks after people's money (4)
10 Dogs can wag this (4)
11 Circular (5)
13 A cover for a jar (3)
15 Sharp barking sound (3)

Across
5 Large, soft feather (5)
6 Underwater boat (3)
7 Bad dream (9)
8 Someone who offers to do something (9)
11 Use oars to move a boat (3)
12 Injury (5)

Down
1 What a door is when you can walk through it (4)
2 A one-floor house (8)
3 You might wear this to hold your trousers up (4)
4 If you can do something, you are ___ to do it (4)
6 Disgraceful (8)
8 Extremely, as in "she was ___ happy" (4)
9 What you might read in a daily paper (4)
10 Something you might go on at a theme park (4)

Across

4 Desert waterhole (5)
6 Someone who isn't telling the truth (4)
7 Pull one vehicle with another (3)
9 African big cat with a spotted coat (7)
10 Drink slowly, like you might with a cup of tea (3)
12 Object (4)
13 Storybook (5)

Down

1 Sadness (6)
2 Set of sports clothes (3)
3 The bad guy in a story (7)
5 Someone who is in the army (7)
8 Without any difficulty (6)
11 Peas grow in this (3)

Across

- **1** Biscuit leftovers (6)
- **4** Soft covering on a dog or other animal (3)
- **5** Above (4)
- **7** Christmas month (abbr) (3)
- **10** Building where a family live (5)
- **11** Movement of a dog's tail (3)
- **13** Small room that moves up and down a building (4)
- **16** Small, crawling insect that lives in large groups (3)
- **17** Bunny (6)

Down

- **1** Shed tears (3)
- **2** Alien spaceship (inits) (3)
- **3** Powerful (6)
- **4** Enemy (3)
- **6** What can be seen from a particular place (4)
- **7** US money (6)
- **8** Restaurant cook (4)
- **9** Put your arms around someone (3)
- **12** Works of creative imagination (3)
- **14** Keyboard button used to jump to the next column (3)
- **15** An article of clothing for the head (3)

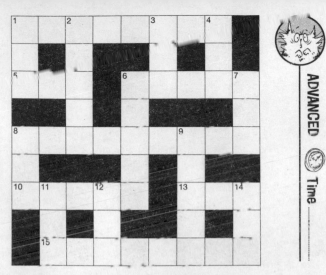

Across

1 Orange-coloured fish often kept as a pet (8)
5 A group of related items (3)
6 What you shed when you cry (5)
8 Jam made with oranges or lemons (9)
10 Young person (5)
13 Strange; unusual (3)
15 "Rubbish!" (8)

Down

1 Elements can be a solid, a liquid or a ___ (3)
2 At some time in the future (5)
3 Frozen water (3)
4 That girl's (3)
6 Rubbish, to an American (5)
7 Try to get money from someone through a legal process; also a girl's name (3)
8 Might (3)
9 Nut from an oak tree (5)
11 Possess (3)
12 The number of fingers and thumbs you have (3)
14 Expected to arrive (3)

Time

Across

1 Horse's foot (4)
4 Stolen treasure (4)
7 Piece of paper in a book (4)
8 Melody (4)
9 Folding beach seat (9)
12 Not tame (4)
14 Unable to feel (4)
16 No longer alive (4)
17 Period of 365 days (4)

Down

1 Part of your thigh (3)
2 Small spot of a different colour to its surroundings (5)
3 Note down quickly (3)
5 Large brass instrument (4)
6 Listen (4)
9 Sunrise (4)
10 Not warm at all (4)
11 Useful (5)
13 Water drops found on grass in the morning (3)
15 Counter where adults buy drinks (3)

ADVANCED 🕐 Time ....

Across

5 A photo or illustration, for example (5)
6 Gear wheel (3)
7 Fierce storm with strong winds (9)
8 Dark-coloured thrush (9)
11 Orang-utan or gorilla (3)
12 Thick milk, sometimes added to coffee (5)

Down

1 Deep breath of relief or sadness (4)
2 Wedding ceremony (8)
3 Mythical hairy snow monster (4)
4 Large, cruel giant (4)
6 Woodwind instrument (8)
8 Ship (4)
9 Hit with your foot (4)
10 Tall, round roof (4)

ADVANCED

Time

Across
- **4** Foolish person (5)
- **6** Long, pointed animal tooth (4)
- **7** For what reason? (3)
- **9** Strong material made from cow's skin (7)
- **10** Word used to connect the last two items in a list (3)
- **12** Specific day (4)
- **13** Musical party (5)

Down
- **1** Picture puzzle where you must assemble the pieces (6)
- **2** Plant seeds in the ground (3)
- **3** Flower wreath (7)
- **5** Wanting a drink (7)
- **8** Dark area behind something lit by the Sun (6)
- **11** Not very intelligent (3)

Across

1 Stitch together with a needle and thread (3)
3 The tip of a pen (3)
5 Had some food (3)
7 Deep hole in the ground (3)
8 What you turn to steer a vehicle (5)
10 Large, poisonous, hairy spider (9)
13 Clothing for your feet (5)
16 Cuddly toy (abbr) (3)
18 A rock with metal in it (3)
19 Public-transport vehicle (3)
20 A long, thin stick, such as one used for fishing (3)

Down

1 Juice inside a tree (3)
2 Extremely common transparent liquid (5)
3 The opposite of old (3)
4 Honey-making insect (3)
6 Small, jumping insect (4)
9 Wooden shelter (3)
10 Exam (4)
11 Noah's ship for pairs of animals (3)
12 Say (5)
14 Taxi (3)
15 "Emergency!" (inits) (3)
17 Disc with a film or TV show on it (inits) (3)

Time

Across

1 Outdoor meal (6)
4 A long way (3)
5 One of the three primary painting colours (4)
7 The opposite of no (3)
10 Type of delicate pottery (5)
11 Not at all wet (3)
13 Small, light-brown songbird (4)
16 Climbing evergreen plant, often seen attached to buildings (3)
17 Something used to harm people in battle (6)

Down

1 Be nosy (3)
2 Young tiger, lion or bear (3)
3 Small, dark red fruit on a stalk with a stone in its centre (6)
4 Payment; charge (3)
6 Guide people by walking ahead (4)
7 Lemon colour (6)
8 Mark left after an injury has healed (4)
9 Tell a lie (3)
12 Thin beam of sunlight (3)
14 Short sleep (3)
15 Come first in a race (3)
ll ow root vegetable (7)

Across

1 A group of letters with a meaning (4)
4 Kitchen, lounge or hall, for example (4)
7 Indian style of meditation (4)
8 A cube used to pick a number from 1 to 6 (4)
9 Washing powder (9)
12 Loose earth (4)
14 Cry of pain (4)
16 Inner part of your hand (4)
17 The opposite of entrance (4)

Down

1 When asking directions, you might say "which ___ do I go?" (3)
2 Male duck (5)
3 Edible fish, often served with chips (3)
5 Small rodents (4)
6 The opposite of right (4)
9 How much of a medicine you should take (4)
10 Short journey (4)
11 Small garden ornament with a beard and pointed hat (5)
13 Not strict (3)
15 Something which has been a big success (3)

Across

5 Hard cereal seed, such as wheat (5)
6 Grown-up boys (3)
7 Model of a person used to scare birds away from crops (9)
8 Strong, spinning column of air (9)
11 Prepaid return envelope (inits) (3)
12 Sharp part of a knife (5)

Down

1 Gets older (4)
2 A heavenly place (8)
3 Just the one time (4)
4 White flakes that fall from the sky (4)
6 Mouldable foodstuff made from almonds and sugar (8)
8 A genie might give you three of these (4)
9 Lower part of the ear (4)
10 Fast, graceful animal with antlers (4)

Across

4 Bread maker (5)
6 What your bedroom might be called if it isn't tidy (4)
7 Used a spade (3)
9 Whirlwind (7)
10 Part of the body between the feet and the hips (3)
12 Sticky material on a roll (4)
13 Relating to a king or queen (5)

Down

1 Soak up liquid (6)
2 Guided, as in a group of people (3)
3 Rain, snow and wind, for example (7)
5 He pulls Santa's sleigh (7)
8 Old, heavily protected building (6)
11 Obtained (3)

	1	2		3		4		5	
	6						7		8
9			10			11		12	
13	14		15						
	16								

Across

- **1** Words spoken by people (8)
- **6** Abroad (8)
- **9** The day before today (9)
- **13** It's used for protection from the rain (8)
- **16** Colourful countryside bird with a long tail (8)

Down

- **2** Higher up than (5)
- **3** Someone staying in a hotel (5)
- **4** Donkey (3)
- **5** Extended period of time (3)
- **7** Word sometimes used to close a story, as in "The ___" (3)
- **8** Place where pigs live (3)
- **9** Not me, but ___ (3)
- **10** Cry uncontrollably (3)
- **11** Turns over and over, as a ball does when it is moving along the ground (5)
- **12** Once more (5)
- **14** Paper representation of the roads and land in an area (3)
- **15** Really regret (3)

Across

1 Someone who delivers letters (7)
6 WALL-E's love (3)
7 Welsh breed of dog (5)
8 Someone who travels into space (9)
10 A minor actor who doesn't usually speak (5)
12 Take advantage of (3)
13 The here and now (7)

Down

1 Titles of nobility (8)
2 Bed covering (5)
3 Machine to "zap" food in (9)
4 Word that's a counterpart to "neither" (3)
5 Healing skin cream (8)
9 Entertain someone and make them laugh (5)
11 Gentle touch (3)

ADVANCED

Time

Across

1 Jump on one foot (3)
3 Sailor's map (5)
6 Father Christmas (5)
7 In cricket, if you get stumped then you are ___ (3)
8 Poisonous mushroom-like plant (9)
9 Mischievous pixie (3)
10 Fried potato snack (5)
12 Odour (5)
13 Long, smooth, cylindrical fish (3)

Down

1 Possesses (3)
2 Large tropical fruit with tough, spiky skin (9)
3 To do with the ancient Greeks or Romans (9)
4 Say sorry (9)
5 Sum up (5)
8 Excursions (5)
11 Buddy (3)

Across

1 Edible fish that's sometimes bought in cans (4)
4 Put your belongings in a bag, ready for a trip (4)
7 It might be grizzly, polar or teddy (4)
8 Portable shelter used when camping (4)
9 It comes on rolls and is used to decorate walls (9)
12 Handle a situation successfully (4)
14 Insects (4)
16 Store a document on a computer (4)
17 Water that falls from the sky (4)

Down

1 Something you bathe in (3)
2 Fool's Day month (5)
3 Perform on stage (3)
5 Hold on to (4)
6 One of many points of light in the night sky (4)
9 String inside a candle (4)
10 There are two of these at the entrance to your mouth (4)
11 One of the three traffic light colours (5)
13 Part of the body used for listening (3)
15 Break a law, especially a religious one (3)

Across

4 A fully grown person (5)
6 Part of a bird used for flying (4)
7 Thick mist (3)
9 Sports shoe with rubber sole (7)
10 The air above you (3)
12 Sensible (4)
13 Large bird that is a symbol of the USA (5)

Down

1 South American, leopard-like wildcat (6)
2 Legolas, in "Lord of the Rings" (3)
3 Something incorrect (7)
5 Somebody who is just visiting a place (7)
8 Reply to a question (6)
11 Tropical potato-like vegetable (3)

Puzzle 117

Across

1 Used to exist (3)
3 TV commercials (3)
5 Succeeded at a competition (3)
7 Brewed leaf drink (3)
8 Medium-sized sailing boat (5)
10 Ninth month (9)
13 Juicy tropical fruit (5)
16 Not switched on (3)
18 "Once upon a time, a long time ___" (3)
19 Pan used to make stir-fried food (3)
20 Common family pet (3)

Down

1 The opposite of dry (3)
2 A bog or marsh (5)
3 At all, as in "is never ___ good" (3)
4 Sixtieth of a minute (abbr) (3)
6 Famous actor (4)
9 A goal or target (3)
10 Japanese wrestling (4)
11 Playground game where one person chases the rest (3)
12 Red liquid flowing around your body (5)
14 At this time (3)
15 Large tree with acorns (3)
17 Soft, pear-shaped fruit with many small seeds (3)

Across

1 Run very fast (6)
4 Large expanse of water between countries (3)
5 Firm hold (4)
7 Male equivalent of "her" (3)
10 Symbol used to indicate subtraction (5)
11 Tool used for scraping weeds (3)
13 Fury (4)
16 Not happy (3)
17 Burn a surface (6)

Down

1 Observed (3)
2 Thick blanket for the floor (3)
3 Walk quietly with your heels raised up (6)
4 Narrow runner for use on snow (3)
6 Go quickly; hurry (4)
7 Red playing card suit (6)
8 Feeling too pleased with oneself (4)
9 The smallest whole number above zero (3)
12 Advanced in years (3)
14 Make a mistake (3)
15 A type of tree, mountain ___ (3)

Puzzle 119

Across

5 Call, usually with a handheld device (5)
6 Secretly watch someone (3)
7 Type of small orange (9)
8 High-ranking teacher (9)
11 Formal title for a knight (3)
12 A word that means "related to the ear" (5)

Down

1 Pimple (4)
2 Heavy fall of rain (8)
3 In this location (4)
4 Over-the-top publicity (4)
6 Tool used for cutting paper (8)
8 Annoying person (4)
9 Academic test (4)
10 Move on wheels (4)

Across

1 Mountaintop (4)
4 Cereal commonly used for food (4)
7 Sweet, brown, fizzy drink (4)
8 Natural underground chamber (4)
9 Medical care given to a patient (9)
12 Propel yourself through water (4)
14 Chair (4)
16 Cab (4)
17 Large town (4)

Down

1 Type of large company with public shares (inits) (3)
2 Furry Australian animal that eats eucalyptus leaves (5)
3 Abbreviation for "and other similar things" (3)
5 Not in any danger (4)
6 Lamb or beef, for example (4)
9 Long, pointed tooth of an elephant (4)
10 Change (4)
11 It might be pop or classical, for example (5)
13 Grown-up male (3)
15 Attempt (3)

Puzzle 121

Across

1 Cow's meat (4)
4 Tint; colour (3)
5 Large, flightless bird that's native to Australia (3)
6 Police officer (3)
8 Engine (5)
9 When the tide goes out, it is said to ___ (3)
10 Sum some numbers (3)
11 Large vehicle for moving goods (5)
13 A common word you use to specify a particular object, instead of "a" or "an" (3)

15 Bird that calls "too-wit too-woo" (3)
16 The Earth orbits this (3)
17 Present (4)

Down

1 Number one (4)
2 Travel to and ___ (3)
3 Say again (6)
4 Modest (6)
6 Wax colouring stick (6)
7 Oar used to row a canoe (6)
12 Take a break (4)
14 Ugly old woman (3)

ADVANCED

Time ......

Across
1 Secret login characters (8)
5 Sound made by a sheep (3)
6 Woodwind instrument (5)
8 Autograph (9)
10 Rely upon (5)
13 Re-voice the sound on a film (3)
15 Was curious about something (8)

Down
1 Place where adults buy drinks (3)
2 Informal language (5)
3 Black, liquid fuel extracted from the ground (3)
4 A small mark, such as a full stop (3)
6 Special meal with lots of food for many people (5)
7 Lamb's mother (3)
8 Rest on a chair (3)
9 The opposite of over (5)
11 A straight line of items (3)
12 Daughter's opposite? (3)
14 The place you sleep (3)

Puzzle 123

Across

1 Creamy frozen dessert (3,5)
6 Unusual (8)
9 Tried (9)
13 Trader; someone who buys and sells things (8)
16 You type on this (8)

Down

2 Find out how many there are of something (5)
3 Two-wheeled vehicle (5)
4 Tree whose name is an anagram of "Mel" (3)
5 Sound made by a cow (3)
7 You might wipe your feet on this (3)
8 Head motion used for agreeing (3)
9 It's between your shoulder and your hand (3)
10 Road-surfacing mixture (3)
11 Instrument with black and white keys (5)
12 Go in (5)
14 Large type of deer (3)
15 Shy or modest (3)

Across
- **4** Perfect (5)
- **6** Poke or jab (4)
- **7** Bite sharply, like a dog might do (3)
- **9** Tool used to tighten bolts (7)
- **10** "Harry Potter" character, Weasley (3)
- **12** British nobleman (4)
- **13** At no time in the past or future (5)

Down
- **1** Capture and hold to ransom (6)
- **2** Metal dish with a handle, used for cooking (3)
- **3** The process of wearing away via natural forces (7)
- **5** Book-lending location (7)
- **8** Put in (6)
- **11** The back part of a football goal (3)

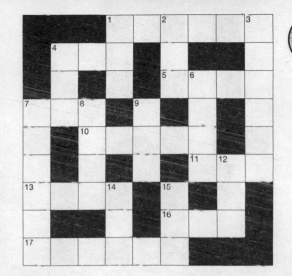

Across

1 Occurring every year (6)
4 Pull behind (3)
5 Symbol used to indicate addition (4)
7 Float gently up and down in water (3)
10 Quarrel; disagree (5)
11 Loud noise (3)
13 Woman (4)
16 Cut and dried grass (3)
17 Picture permanently inked into the skin (6)

Down

1 Amazement (3)
2 Short sleep (3)
3 Learning period (6)
4 Noah's per-species limit (3)
6 Didn't tell the truth (4)
7 Type of gymnastic dance (6)
8 Musical group (4)
9 Shelled food often eaten fried, scrambled or boiled (3)
12 Climbing vine (3)
14 "Are we there ___?" (3)
15 Classic game, "Guess ___?" (3)

Across

5 Small garden creature that leaves a shiny trail (5)
6 Elderly person (inits) (3)
7 Tree that stays in leaf all year long (9)
8 Exactly the same (9)
11 Permit someone to do something (3)
12 Make someone unhappy (5)

Down

1 Guernsey or Jersey, for example (4)
2 Hard road edge for people to walk along (8)
3 Banner flown to show your allegiance (4)
4 The opposite of shut (4)
6 Cloudy (8)
8 Sitting around doing nothing (4)
9 Genuine; honest (4)
10 Overdue (4)

Time

Across

1 Bonfire-night month (8)
5 A score of zero (3)
6 The position between ninth and eleventh (5)
8 Roman warrior who fought in public displays (9)
10 Follow someone's movements (5)
13 Rule that applies throughout a country (3)
15 Small, freshwater turtle (8)

Down

1 Mother Teresa was one (3)
2 Large country house, especially in Roman times (5)
3 The opposite of hello (3)
4 Turn bad, like fruit (3)
6 Magic routine (5)
7 Female equivalent of "his" (3)
8 Understand, like a joke (3)
9 Colourful spring flower that grows from a bulb (5)
11 Dull habit that's hard to change (3)
12 Motor vehicle (3)
14 Looking tired or pale (3)

Across
1 Fall downwards (4)
4 Parent's sister (4)
7 Night-sky object that causes the tides (4)
8 Give a title to something (4)
9 A way to cook eggs (9)
12 Applaud (4)
14 A curved structure over an opening (4)
16 Attic (4)
17 Something a plant grows from (4)

Down
1 Block the flow of water (3)
2 Black-and-white, bear-like animal found in China (5)
3 Small hotel (3)
5 The opposite of short (4)
6 Repair (4)
9 Item of clothing for your foot (4)
10 Not imaginary (4)
11 Water transports (5)
13 Burst, like a balloon (3)
15 Concealed (3)

ADVANCED

Time ....

Puzzle 129

Across

- **4** Not yet written on (5)
- **6** Free from bias (4)
- **7** Family; relatives (3)
- **9** Bird with large, colourful fan like tail (7)
- **10** Because of (3)
- **12** All of the time from birth until death (4)
- **13** Someone who assists a doctor (5)

Down

- **1** In a foreign country (6)
- **2** Liquid used for writing (3)
- **3** Spear used to catch whales (7)
- **5** Start time at a football match (4-3)
- **8** Powder from flowers (6)
- **11** What Aladdin had to do to the lamp to make the genie appear (3)

Time

Across

1 Short unit of time (abbr) (3)
3 The whole lot (3)
5 Go slowly and not keep up with the rest (3)
7 Shout of disapproval (3)
8 Central arm joint (5)
10 Each person (9)
13 Tree supports (5)
16 Unwell (3)
18 As well (3)
19 Period of 24 hours (3)
20 Repeatedly pester someone (3)

Down

1 Replacement player during a game (abbr) (3)
2 Shut (5)
3 This number is how old you are (3)
4 Place that scientists work (3)
6 Opposite of home, in football (4)
9 Throw in a high arc (3)
10 European currency (4)
11 Rodent that resembles a large mouse (3)
12 Round vegetable with a strong smell (5)
14 The opposite of even (3)
15 Pig's house (3)
17 Large piece of wood cut from a tree (3)

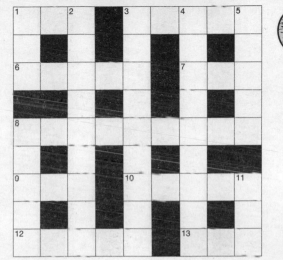

Across

1 Drink with the tongue (3)
3 Raw vegetable dish (5)
6 Strong claw, found on a bird of prey (5)
7 Container for storing rubbish (3)
8 Flying vehicle with wings and an engine (9)
9 Mince ___, tart eaten at Christmas (3)
10 Cost (5)
12 Mistake (5)
13 Cashew or macadamia, for example (3)

Down

1 A large number or amount (3)
2 Large, white, Arctic creature (5,4)
3 Rough sheet used to smooth wood (9)
4 Someone who helps you borrow books (9)
5 Waltz or tango, for example (5)
8 Crunchy green or red fruit (5)
11 Chew and swallow (3)

ADVANCED

Time

Across

5 Wide (5)
6 Purchase an item (3)
7 The Queen's name (9)
8 It can be milk, dark or white (9)
11 Vehicle some children catch to school (3)
12 You need this to bite (5)

Down

1 Woodwind instrument (4)
2 Game with dotted tiles representing numbers (8)
3 Brainwave (4)
4 Legend (4)
6 Animal that hunts other animals (8)
8 The shape of a dice (4)
9 Not fooled by; "I'm __ __ you" (2,2)
10 A sound that repeats (4)

Puzzle 133

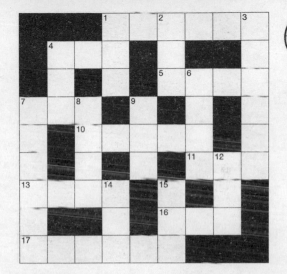

Across
1 In the land of nod (6)
4 Piece of wood used for rowing (3)
5 Device for catching animals (4)
7 Common vegetable that grows in a pod (3)
10 Man marrying a bride (5)
11 Animal kept at home (3)
13 Final (4)
16 Tennis serve winner (3)
17 Heaviness (6)

Down
1 Drawings, paintings, sculptures and music (3)
2 Old light (3)
3 Doll controlled by hand, sometimes with strings (6)
4 Mineral-bearing rock (3)
6 Man-made slope (4)
7 Cushion for sleeping on (6)
8 "A really long time!" (4)
9 Came first in a race (3)
12 Two of these are used when you look at the world (3)
14 Label attached to a present (3)
15 It's used to play baseball (3)

ADVANCED

Time

Across
4 Music and sound (5)
6 Turn over quickly (4)
7 Put a question to (3)
9 Hair on an animal's face (7)
10 Slightly mocking, as in "a ___ smile" (3)
12 Pleasant and agreeable (4)
13 Type of silky material (5)

Down
1 Serviette (6)
2 Going through; stopping at (3)
3 Comes into bloom (7)
5 Large bird that can run fast but can't fly (7)
8 Thin (6)
11 Long-haired ox (3)

Puzzle 135

Across
1 The opposite of "girls" (4)
4 Stretched tight (4)
7 Low-pitch musical instrument (4)
8 Large plant with a trunk (4)
9 Time between morning and evening (9)
12 Quacking bird (4)
14 Remove creases from clothing (4)
16 Man crowned as ruler (4)
17 Parsley, sage or thyme, for example (4)

Down
1 Word used to introduce a contrasting viewpoint (3)
2 Not fresh, perhaps (5)
3 A small wound (3)
5 Threesome; anagram of "riot" (4)
6 Plant with green, feathery leaves and fronds (4)
9 Sums numbers together (4)
10 Mark used when something is correct (4)
11 Horse's whinny (5)
13 Sports outfit (3)
15 Pen point (3)

Across

1 All the letters in a language (8)
5 Adult males (3)
6 An elephant's nose (5)
8 Go along with (9)
10 Bronze medal position (5)
13 Powerful boat used for pulling ships (3)
15 False teeth (8)

Down

1 Point at a target (3)
2 Overwhelming fear (5)
3 Metal pole (3)
4 Stay in the sun to darken your skin (3)
6 Shy; easily scared (5)
7 It's used to open a lock (3)
8 Suitable in the circumstances (3)
9 Make a change (5)
11 Did own (3)
12 Sprint (3)
14 Air-like substance (3)

Across

1 A type of computer made by Apple (3)

3 Special person; celebrity (inits) (3)

5 You would use this if you wanted to cut down a tree (3)

7 Precious stone (3)

8 Tall, narrow building (5)

10 Female ballet dancer (9)

13 Large, stringed instrument (5)

16 Confess to something: ___ up (3)

18 Period of fighting between armies (3)

19 Artificial colour (3)

20 Twist around a vertical axis, as an aeroplane does (3)

Down

1 Large cup (3)

2 Desert animal with one or two humps and long eyelashes (5)

3 Animal doctor (3)

4 Dog's foot (3)

6 Region or space, as in "that's part of the play ___" (4)

9 Belonging to us (3)

10 Rear surface (4)

11 Text-speak laugh (inits) (3)

12 White piano keys used to be made of this (5)

14 Top (3)

15 Have an obligation to repay something (3)

17 Not previously existing (3)

Time ......

Across
1 Colourful hair accessory (6)
4 Stick your nose in (3)
5 Group or society (4)
7 Foot extremity (3)
10 Snake poison (5)
11 Young man (3)
13 Put a liquid in (4)
16 Biblical vessel (3)
17 Other than, as in "I want them all, ___ for that" (6)

Down
1 A cereal plant; an anagram of "rey" (3)
2 TV channel that shows "Doctor Who" (inits) (3)
3 Not anyone (6)
4 In favour of (3)
6 An arm or leg (4)
7 Pudding made with custard, cream, fruit and sponge (6)
8 The opposite of good (4)
9 Small, crawling insect (3)
12 Type of tree that produces acorns (3)
14 Not tell the truth (3)
15 Sales tax (inits) (3)

ADVANCED Time

Across

4 White cooking powder (5)
6 Not a single one (4)
7 A pile of blank paper fastened together in a book (3)
9 A red sauce you might have with chips (7)
10 Limb used for walking on (3)
12 Govern (4)
13 Poisonous (5)

Down

1 Number halfway between ten and thirty (6)
2 Fast-spoken music (3)
3 Short printed publication (7)
5 Immature frog (7)
8 Christian building of worship (6)
11 Almighty being (3)

Time

Across

1 Mixture of smoke and fog (4)
4 The clear part of spectacles (4)
7 "Star Wars" Jedi master (4)
8 The opposite of up (4)
9 A letter of the alphabet that isn't a vowel (9)
12 Quick (4)
14 Make music with your voice (4)
16 Pie containing jam (4)
17 Scream at someone (4)

Down

1 Nervous in public (3)
2 Windows are made of this (5)
3 A joining word, as in "this ___ that" (3)
5 Settee (4)
6 Tangle in a piece of string or rope (4)
9 A place selling food and drink (4)
10 A bird's home (4)
11 Not very nice at all (5)
13 Money that must be paid to the government (3)
15 Substance used to style hair (3)

ADVANCED ⏱ Time ....

Across

1 Stick out (3)
3 Something that is true (4)
5 Female parent (3)
6 Maths puzzle (3)
8 Circular Italian bread dish (5)
9 Female rabbit (3)
10 Word used to form a negative (3)
11 Knight's weapon (5)
13 Place something somewhere, as in ___ down (3)
15 Assistance; help (3)
17 You might say this if you stub your toe! (4)
18 Parent's boy (3)

Down

1 Fruity spread (3)
2 Violent storm (7)
3 What a drink of cola does when poured into a glass (4)
4 The day before Friday (abbr) (3)
6 Strapped shoes, sometimes worn in summer (7)
7 Came across someone (3)
9 Quick swim (3)
12 A sworn promise (4)
14 Flying saucer (inits) (3)
16 Lair (3)

ADVANCED

Time ....

Across

- **5** Avoid (5)
- **6** Produce an egg, if you're a hen (3)
- **7** Short-tailed game bird (9)
- **8** Police officer (9)
- **11** Morse code emergency (inits) (3)
- **12** "L"-size clothing (5)

Down

- **1** Aid (4)
- **2** Jewellery pair (8)
- **3** Rip (4)
- **4** Computer memory unit (4)
- **6** Red and black spotted beetle (8)
- **8** Carry bag (4)
- **9** Cash register (4)
- **10** Number that's wholly divisible by two (4)

Across

1 Silly; ridiculous (6)
4 Shoot with a laser gun (3)
5 Happy (4)
7 Long-handled gardening tool (3)
10 Large, shrimp-like shellfish (5)
11 Somewhere people go to keep fit (3)
13 The unusually long part of a giraffe's body (4)
16 The narrow end of something (3)
17 Get messily twisted together (6)

Down

1 Large, tailless monkey (3)
2 Droop down in the middle (3)
3 Bumper car (6)
4 Animal park (3)
6 Measuring a great distance (4)
7 Large wasp (6)
8 A story of heroic adventure (4)
9 The opposite of good (3)
12 The sound a small dog makes when it barks (3)
14 Small barrel (3)
15 Had dinner, perhaps (3)

Time

Across

4 Room just under the roof of a house (5)
6 An animal's sharp, curved nail (4)
7 Cardboard container (3)
9 Unusual; different (7)
10 Work done for money (3)
12 Plants hidden microphones (4)
13 Iron, silver or copper, for example (5)

Down

1 Solicitor; expert in legal matters (6)
2 Not tell the truth (3)
3 Flower on a fruit tree (7)
5 Sixth-form school, perhaps (7)
8 Able to move quickly (6)
11 Put money on the result of a game (3)

Level Four:
Ace Puzzlers

Puzzle 145

ACE PUZZLERS

Across

7 One-person boat (5)
8 The Amazon, Thames or Nile, for example (5)
9 Strong feeling (7)
10 Door-bashing device, battering ___ (3)
11 Leg-to-foot joint (5)
13 All of a group (5)
15 Letters you might find written on a gravestone (inits) (3)
17 Colourful sky display (7)
20 Circus performer with bright red nose (5)
21 Christmas hymn (5)

Down

1 A steady pain (4)
2 Open a door with a key (6)
3 The Abominable Snowman (4)
4 A common citrus fruit (6)
5 Walkie-talkie sign-off (4)
6 Bad-tempered (6)
11 One of the continents (6)
12 Small job, chore (6)
14 Glowing remains of a fire (6)
16 Object used on stage in a theatre (4)
18 In length units, there are twelve of these in a foot (4)
19 Wild animal that's like a big dog (4)

Puzzle 146

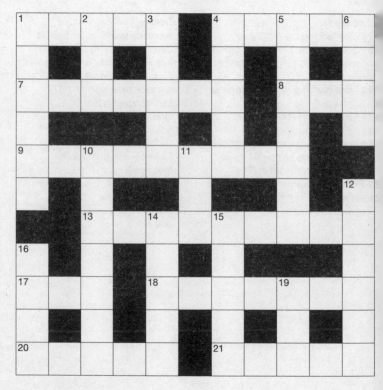

Across

Poisonous snake (5)

Plant with red flowers, often associated with peace after war (5)

A, B and C are ___ (7)

Scoring play in rugby (3)

Citrus fruit preserve (9)

13 Long, stringy pasta (9)

17 Small house or shelter (3)

18 Person who gives the lessons at school (7)

20 What you walk on (5)

21 Large wildcat with black stripes (5)

Down

1 Pillar, often found in Greek and Roman ruins (6)

2 Closed the teeth on something (3)

3 Somewhere sports events take place (5)

4 Italian noodles (5)

5 Happy to wait (7)

6 Toy that goes up and down on a string (2-2)

10 Sticky rice dish (7)

11 Carry or drag something heavy (3)

12 Reflecting glass (6)

14 Later in time (5)

15 Blood-pumping organ (5)

16 Professional cook (4)

19 Male pig (3)

Puzzle 147

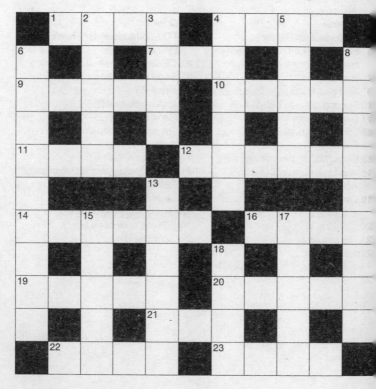

150 **151**

152 **153**

Ace Puzzlers

145

146

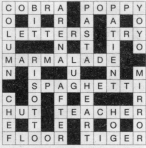

147

148

149

140

```
S M O G . . A . .
H . . L E N S . K
Y O D A . D O W N
. . . S . . F . O
C O N S O N A N T
A . E . A . . . .
F A S T . S I N G
E . T A R T . . E
. . X . Y E L L .
```

141

```
J U T . F A C T .
A . E . I . . H .
M U M . Z . S U M
. . P I Z Z A . E
D O E . . . N O T
I . S W O R D . .
P U T . A . A I D
. F . . T . L . E
. O U C H . S O N
```

142

```
H . E . I . . . B
E V A D E . L A Y
L . R . A . A . T
P A R T R I D G E
. . I . . . Y . .
C O N S T A B L E
A . G . I . I . V
S O S . L A R G E
E . . . L . D . N
```

143

```
. . . A B S U R D
. Z A P . A . . O
. O . E . G L A D
H O E . B . O . G
O . P R A W N . E
R . I . D . G Y M
N E C K . A . A .
E . . E . T I P .
T A N G L E . . .
```

144

```
. . . L . . F . .
. B . A T T I C .
C L A W . . B O X
. O . Y . N . L .
. S P E C I A L .
. S . R . M . E .
J O B . . B U G S
. M E T A L . E .
. . T . . E . . .
```

134

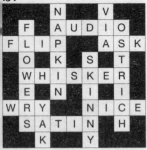

135

136

137

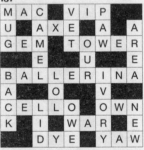

138

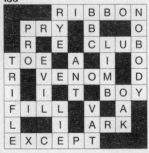

139

128

D	R	O	P		I		
A			A	U	N	T		M
M	O	O	N		N	A	M	E
			D		L		N
S	C	R	A	M	B	L	E	D
O		E			O		
C	L	A	P		A	R	C	H
K		L	O	F	T			I
		P		S	E	E	D

129

		A			I	
	H	B	L	A	N	K
F	A	I	R		K	I	N
	R	O		P		C
	P	E	A	C	O	C	K
	O		D	L		O
F	O	R			L	I	F	E
N	U	R	S	E		F

130

S	E	C		A	L	L	
U		L	A	G		A		A
B	O	O		E	L	B	O	W
		S		O			A
E	V	E	R	Y	B	O	D	Y
U		A		N		
R	O	O	T	S		I	L	L
O		D		T	O	O		O
	D	A	Y		N	A	G

131

L	A	P		S	A	L	A	D
O		O		A		I		A
T	A	L	O	N		B	I	N
		A		D		R		C
A	E	R	O	P	L	A	N	E
P		B		A		R	
P	I	E		P	R	I	C	E
L		A		E		A		A
E	R	R	O	R		N	U	T

132

O		D		I			M
B	R	O	A	D		P	A	Y
O		M		E		R		T
E	L	I	Z	A	B	E	T	H
		N			D		
C	H	O	C	O	L	A	T	E
U		E		N		T		C
B	U	S		T	O	O	T	H
E			O		R		O

133

		A	S	L	E	E	P
	O	A	R		I		U
	R		T		T	R	A	P
P	E	A		W		A		P
I		G	R	O	O	M		E
L		E		N		P	E	T
L	A	S	T		B		Y
O		A		A	C	E
W	E	I	G	H	T

122

```
P A S S W O R D █
U █ L █ █ I █ O █
B A A █ F L U T E
█ █ N █ E █ █ █ W
S I G N A T U R E
I █ █ █ S █ N █ █
T R U S T █ D U B
█ O █ O █ █ E █ E
█ W O N D E R E D
```

123

```
I C E C R E A M █
█ O █ Y █ L █ O █
█ U N C O M M O N
█ N █ L █ A █ O █
A T T E M P T E D
R █ A █ █ I █ N █
M E R C H A N T █
█ L █ O █ N █ E █
█ K E Y B O A R D
```

124

```
█ █ K █ P █ █ █ █
█ E █ I D E A L █
P R O D █ N I P █
O █ N █ I █ B █ █
S P A N N E R █ █
I █ P █ S █ A █ █
R O N █ █ E A R L
█ N E V E R █ Y █
█ █ T █ █ T █ █ █
```

125

```
█ █ A N N U A L █
█ T O W █ A █ E █
█ W █ E █ P L U S
B O B █ E █ I █ S
A █ A R G U E █ O
L █ N █ G █ D I N
L A D Y █ W █ V █
E █ █ E █ H A Y █
T A T T O O █ █ █
```

126

```
I █ P █ F █ █ █ O
S N A I L █ O A P
L █ V █ A █ V █ E
E V E R G R E E N
█ █ M █ █ R █ █ █
I D E N T I C A L
D █ N █ R █ A █ A
L E T █ U P S E T
E █ █ █ E █ T █ E
```

127

```
N O V E M B E R █
U █ I █ █ Y █ O █
N I L █ T E N T H
█ █ L █ R █ █ E █
G L A D I A T O R
E █ █ C █ U █ █ █
T R A C K █ L A W
█ U █ A █ I █ A █
█ T E R R A P I N
```

116

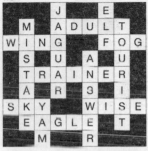

```
. . J . . E . .
. M . A D U L T
W I N G . . F O G
. S . U . A . U
. T R A I N E R .
. A . R . 3 . I
S K Y . . W I S E
. E A G L E . T
. M . . R
```

117

```
W A S . A D S .
E . W O N . E . S
T E A . Y A C H T
. . M . . I . . A
S E P T E M B E R
U . . A . . L .
M A N G O . O F F
N . O . A G O . I
. W O K . D O G
```

118

```
. . S P R I N T
. S E A . U . . I
. K . W . G R I P
H I S . O . U . T
E . M I N U S . O
A . U . E . H O E
R A G E . A . L
T . . R . S A D
S C O R C H
```

119

```
S . D . H . . II
P H O N E . S P Y
O . W . R . C . P
T A N G E R I N E
. . P . . . S
P R O F E S S O R
E . U . X . O . O
S I R . A U R A L
T . . M . S . L
```

120

```
P E A K . E
L . . O A T S . M
C O L A . C A V E
. . L . . F . A
T R E A T M E N T
U . D . . U
S W I M . S E A T
K . T A X I . R
. . N . C I T Y
```

121

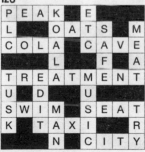

```
. . . B E E F
R . H U E . R
E M U . S . C O P
P . M O T O R . A
E B B . . . A D D
A . L O R R Y . D
T H E . E . O W L
. A . S U N . E
G I F T
```

110

```
A . P . O . . . S
G R A I N . M E N
E . R . C . A . O
S C A R E C R O W
. . D . . Z . . .
W H I R L W I N D
I . S . O . P . E
S A E . B L A D E
H . . E . N . . R
```

111

```
. . A . . L .
. W . B A K E R
M E S S . . D U G
. A . O . C . D .
. T O R N A D O .
. H . B . S . L .
L E G . . T A P E
. R O Y A L . H .
. . T . . E .
```

112

```
L A N G U A G E .
. B . U . S . R .
. O V E R S E A S
. V . S . N . T .
Y E S T E R D A Y
O . O . . O . G .
U M B R E L L A .
. A . U . L . I .
. P H E A S A N T
```

113

```
P O S T M A N .
E . H . I . O . O
E V E . C O R G I
R . E . R . . . N
A S T R O N A U T
G . . W . M . M .
E X T R A . U S E
S . A . V . S . N
. P R E S E N T .
```

114

```
H O P . C H A R T
A . I . L . P . O
S A N T A . O U T
. . E . S . L . A
T O A D S T O O L
R . P . I . G . .
I M P . C R I S P
P . L . A . Z . A
S M E L L . E E L
```

115

```
T U N A . A . .
U . P A C K . S
B E A R . T E N T
. . I . . E . A
W A L L P A P E R
I . I . . M . .
C O P E . B U G S
K . S A V E . . I
. . R . R A I N
```

104

```
H O O F . . J . . .
I . . L O O T . H .
P A G E . . T U N E
. . . C . . B . A .
D E C K C H A I R .
A . O . . ^ . . R .
W I L D . N U M B .
N . D E A D . . A .
. . . W . Y E A R .
```

105

```
S . M . Y . . . O
I M A G E . C O G
G . R . T . L . R
H U R R I C A N E
. . . I . . R . E
B L A C K B I R D
O . G . I . N . O
A P E . C R E A M
T . K . T . . . E
```

106

```
. . J . . . S . .
. G . I D I O T .
F A N G . . W H Y
R . S . S . I . .
. L E A T H E R .
A . W . A . S . .
A N D . . D A T E
. D I S C O . Y .
. . M . . W . . .
```

107

```
S E W . . N I B .
A . A T E . E . F
P I T . W H E E L
. E . . U . L . F
T A R A N T U L A
E . R . T . . . .
S O C K S . T E D
T . A . O R E . V
. B U S . R O D .
```

108

```
. . . P I C N I C
. F A R . U . . H
. E . Y . B L U E
Y E S . F . E . R
E . C H I N A . R
L . A . B . D R Y
L A R K . W . A .
O . I . I V Y . .
W E A P O N . . .
```

109

```
W O R D . C . .
A . R O O M . L
Y O G A . D I C E
. . K . C . F .
D E T E R G E N T
O . R . N . . .
S O I L . O U C H
E . P A L M . I .
. . X . E X I T .
```

98

C	A	T			L	O	A	F	
A		H		O			R	
P	I	E		U		M	O	W
		A	U	D	I	O		I
F	A	T				N	A	G
E		R	O	A	D	S		
D	I	E		R		T	O	Y
	C			E		E		E
	Y	O	D	A		R	A	W

99

H	I	S	S		A			
O			H	I	G	H		S
T	R	I	O		E	A	S	T
			R		L		A	
B	U	T	T	E	R	F	L	Y
A		A		O				
N	A	I	L		U	G	L	Y
K		L	I	O	N			A
		D		D	A	M	P	

100

O		B		B				A
P	L	U	M	E		S	U	B
E		N		L		H		L
N	I	G	H	T	M	A	R	E
		A			M			
V	O	L	U	N	T	E	E	R
E		O		E		F		I
R	O	W		W	O	U	N	D
Y				S		L		E

101

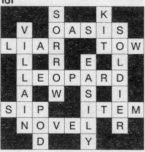

		S			K		
	V		O	A	S	I	S
L	I	A	R			T	O	W
	L		R		E		L
	L	E	O	P	A	R	D
	A		W		S		I
S	I	P			I	T	E	M
	N	O	V	E	L		R
	D			Y		

102

		C	R	U	M	B	S
	F	U	R		F		T
	O		Y		O	V	E	R
D	E	C		H		I		O
O		H	O	U	S	E		N
L		E		G		W	A	G
L	I	F	T		H		R
A			A		A	N	T
R	A	B	B	I	T		

103

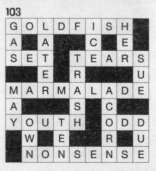

G	O	L	D	F	I	S	H	
A		A			C		E	
S	E	T		T	E	A	R	S
		E		R				U
M	A	R	M	A	L	A	D	E
A			S		C			
Y	O	U	T	H		O	D	D
	W		E		R			U
N	O	N	S	E	N	S	E	

Advanced

93

94

95

96

97

88

	S	U	M	M	E	R
	W		A			U
D	E	F	R	O	S	T
	A				T	
T	R	U	M	P	E	T
A			E		A	
P	A	S	T	E	L	

89

		F			H	
	C	O	S	M	I	C
Y	O	U			G	
	F	L	A	S	H	
	F			H	E	Y
S	E	N	I	O	R	
	E			P		

90

		S	P	A	D	E
	D		A		O	
K	E	T	C	H	U	P
	G		K		B	
T	R	E	A	C	L	E
	E		G		E	
F	E	V	E	R		

91

			P			
	C	H	A	I	R	
	A		R		O	
B	L	O	S	S	O	M
	L		N		T	
	S	A	I	L	S	
			P			

92

L	U	C	K			
I		R		R	O	T
S	T	A	G	E		O
T		T		T		I
E		E	Q	U	A	L
N	O	R		R		E
			G	N	A	T

82

		P			D	
	L	E	T	T	E	R
S	E	A			S	
	G	R	A	P	E	
	E			U	R	N
I	N	S	U	L	T	
	D			L		

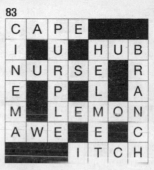

83

C	A	P	E			
I		U		H	U	B
N	U	R	S	E		R
E		P		L		A
M		L	E	M	O	N
A	W	E		E		C
			I	T	C	H

84

I	D	E	A			
	E		N	I	T	
	P		C		A	
V	A	L	I	A	N	T
	R		E		D	
	T	O	N		E	
			T	I	M	E

85

S	I	G	H	T		
E		O		O	L	D
A		G	O	D		O
R	U	G		D	E	N
C		L	O	L		K
H	U	E		E		E
		S	O	R	R	Y

86

		A	G	R	E	E
	H		L		N	
H	O	L	I	D	A	Y
	N		T		M	
K	E	S	T	R	E	L
	S		E		L	
S	T	O	R	Y		

87

	H		C		E	
R	E	V	O	L	V	E
	X		L		E	
S	A	P	L	I	N	G
	G		E		I	
V	O	L	C	A	N	O
	N		T		G	

70

71

72

73

74

75

76

77

78

79

80

81

58

			D		
	F	L	O	A	T
	L	L		A	
C	O	M	P	O	S	T
	C	H		T	
	K	N	I	F	E
		N			

59

G	E	L		S	A	Y
U		O	A	P		A
M	O	B		I	N	K
		S		N		
N	O	T		A	I	D
O		E	T	C		I
W	A	R		H	A	Y

60

	P	U	B	L	I	C
	E		A			U
K	A	R	A	O	K	E
	C				N	
W	E	L	L	I	E	S
A			A		E	
S	Y	M	B	O	L	

61

	C		C		G	
C	A	G	O	U	I	F
	K		N		A	
H	A	R	V	E	S	T
	M		I		S	
T	E	A	C	H	E	R
	L		T		S	

62

		T		A	
	S	A	F	A	R	I
W	A	X			C	
	L	I	G	H	T	
	M			A	I	R
M	O	S	A	I	C	
	N			R		

63

		S	P	A	C	E
	S		R		H	
S	C	O	O	T	E	R
	R		J		E	
R	E	L	E	A	S	E
	A		C		E	
E	M	P	T	Y		

64

		M			
	S	L	E	E	P
	T		R		R
W	A	R	M	S	U	P
	I		A		N
	N	O	I	S	E
		D			

65

S	C	A	R	F	
T		N		R	Y	E
R		T	U	E		X
O	I	L		C	U	P
K		E	L	K		E
E	A	R		L		R
		S	H	E	E	T

66

D	I	S	C	U	S	
I		O		U	
F	L	O	W	E	R	S
N				N	
P	E	L	I	C	A	N
S		N		M	
S	U	N	S	E	T	

67

	D		A		G	
H	O	R	I	Z	O	N
	O		R		S	
T	R	E	M	B	L	E
	M		A		I	
P	A	T	I	E	N	T
	T		L		G	

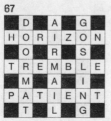

68

	S	P	E	L	L
T	O	E		C	E
I		R	O	L	L	S
N		V		I		S
S	T	A	M	P		O
E		N		S	O	N
L	I	T	R	E	

69

P	A	I	R		
	B		E	G	G
	O		D		A
J	A	N	U	A	R	Y
	R		C		A
	D	Y	E		G
		D	I	E	T

46

```
  P   M   N  
P Y J A M A S
  R   N   U  
S A U S A G E
  M   I   H  
R I S O T T O
  D   N   Y  
```

47

```
  P O T A T O
  R   H   O  
C O L U M N  
  M   N   I  
  I N D I G O
  S   E   H  
S E C R E T  
```

48

```
N A R R O W  
  I   A   E  
T R A G E D Y
  P       D  
N O S T R I L
  R   W   N  
  T R O U G H
```

49

```
T O A D      
I   F   F E W
C O R G I   A
K   I   E   L
E   C A R O L
T E A   C   E
      F E E T
```

50

```
L E A P      
  M   A S H  
  P   P   E  
B I C Y C L E
  R   R   I  
E M U   U    
      S U M S
```

51

```
  U   I   S  
U N U S U A L
  I   R   T  
S C R A T C H
  O   E   H  
T R O L L E Y
  N   I   L  
```

52

```
    P A P E R
F L U   R   E
L   D R E S S
O   D   S   U
W H I T E   L
E   N   N U T
R I G H T    
```

53

```
N O O D L E S
U   C   E   T
M A T   T H U
B   O U T   D
E B B   U S E
R   E   C   N
S E R P E N T
```

54

```
D I E D      
O   X   M O P
C O C O A   A
T   U   R   R
O   S L I D E
R O E   N   N
      H E A T
```

55

```
S W E E T    
T   M   O P T
R   P E A   U
E W E   S O N
E   R A T   N
T O O   E   E
    R U R A L
```

56

```
    S     F  
  F O L L O W
A L L     R  
  Y O U N G  
  I     E E L
I N F E C T  
  G     K    
```

57

```
A W A R D    
B   M   I M P
A R E Ñ A   R
C   R   M   A
U   I V O R Y
S E C   N   E
    A D D E R
```

36

H		S		B
A	M	P	L	E
P		E		A
P	A	N	I	C
Y		D		H

Intermediates

37

	S	C	A	R	E
T	O	P		B		C
E		E	M	A	I	L
N		A		N		A
N	A	K	E	D		I
I		E		O	A	R
S	I	R	E	N		

38

		M		A	
	S	A	D	D	L	E
A		O	T		M	
	H	E	L	L	O	
	O		A	N	Y	
F	O	R	B	I	D	
	L			R		

39

L	A	M	B		G	
	C		O	B	O	E
	C	H	O	I	R	
B	U	Y		I	I	T
	S	M	A	L	L	
S	E	N	D		L	
	D		D	R	A	W

40

P	H	A	N	T	O	M
R		G		I		Y
E	A	T		D	I	S
T		R	O	D		T
E	V	E		L	I	E
N		S		E		R
D	E	S	T	R	O	Y

41

			P			
	P	L	A	T	E	
	A		N		A	
M	U	S	T	A	R	D
	S		H		L	
	E	N	E	M	Y	
			R			

42

	J	E	A	N	S	
W	H	O		D		T
I		U	N	D	E	R
N		R		R		I
D	A	N	C	E		N
O		A		S	A	G
W	A	L	L	S		

43

P	A	S	T	A		
R		E		T	I	E
E	A	R	T	H		R
T		I		L		R
T		O	P	E	R	A
Y	O	U		T		N
		S	P	E	E	D

44

		E		C		
	B	U	C	K	E	T
F	I	R		R		
	G	O	O	S	E	
	G		H	A	S	
P	E	N	C	I	L	
	R			P		

45

E	L	F		T	I	N
L		L	O	W		I
M	O	O		I	L	L
		R		T		
S	K	I		T	U	G
O		S	E	E		A
B	I	T		R	I	P

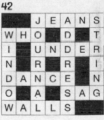

24

P	A	T	H	■
■	L	■	E	■
F	A	I	R	Y
■	R	■	O	■
■	M	E	N	U

25

H	E	A	V	Y
■	R	■	I	■
G	R	A	S	S
■	O	■	I	■
T	R	U	T	H

26

■	S	■	T	■
P	U	P	I	L
■	G	U	T	■
T	A	B	L	E
■	R	■	E	■

27

■	P	I	L	L
■	H	■	A	■
D	O	U	B	T
■	T	■	E	■
F	O	I	L	■

28

■	A	F	A	R
■	I	■	A	■
V	I	X	E	N
O	■	E	■	■
W	A	D	E	■

29

D	I	T	C	H
E	■	I	■	O
N	I	G	H	T
I	■	E	■	E
M	O	R	A	L

30

U	S	U	A	L
■	N	■	G	■
T	O	T	A	L
■	R	■	I	■
B	E	A	N	S

31

C	A	F	E	■
U	■	R	■	S
B	L	E	A	T
E	■	S	■	E
■	C	H	I	P

32

■	T	■	P	■
J	O	K	E	R
■	W	I	T	■
M	E	D	A	L
■	R	■	L	■

33

■	S	T	O	P
■	R	■	A	■
C	H	A	R	T
O	■	I	■	■
T	U	N	A	■

34

D	I	A	R	Y
W	■	L	■	A
A	T	T	I	C
R	■	A	■	H
F	I	R	S	T

35

G	R	O	W	■
■	U	■	O	■
C	L	I	M	B
■	E	■	A	■
■	S	A	N	D

12

B	I	T	E	
A		O		T
C	U	R	R	Y
K		C		P
	S	H	O	E

13

C	O	A	S	T
L		C		E
E	X	T	R	A
A		O		C
N	O	R	T	H

14

	S	H	E	D
		Y		O
T	H	E	F	T
A		N		
R	O	A	D	

15

	S	A	C	K
	O		R	
F	L	O	U	R
	V		S	
N	E	W	T	

16

T	W	I	G	
	H		I	
L	I	A	R	S
	S		L	
	K	I	S	S

17

L	A	C	E	
O		L		G
C	R	A	W	L
K		S		U
	I	S	L	E

18

T		W		J
H	O	R	S	E
I		U		W
C	A	N	O	E
K		G		L

19

G	H	O	S	T
U		F		H
E	N	T	E	R
S		E		E
S	E	N	S	E

20

G	L	O	B	E
	A		O	
T	R	E	A	T
	G		S	
D	E	P	T	H

21

	A	L	S	O
	N		C	
I	G	L	O	O
	E		O	
W	R	A	P	

22

	X	M	A	S
		A		I
A	L	T	E	R
P		H		
T	A	S	K	

23

C	A	P	E	
O		I		M
D	I	Z	Z	Y
E		Z		T
	O	A	T	H

Beginners

1
E	Y	E	S	░
X	░	A	░	D
A	N	G	L	E
M	░	L	░	E
░	W	E	E	P

2
░	C	░	B	░
G	L	O	R	Y
░	O	W	E	░
S	A	L	A	D
░	K	░	D	░

3
B	L	O	O	M
E	░	C	░	O
L	I	E	I	N
C	░	A	░	E
H	O	N	E	Y

4
░	S	T	A	G
░	░	E	░	E
W	H	E	A	T
O	░	T	░	░
E	C	H	O	░

5
░	W	E	S	T
░	H	░	A	░
M	O	V	I	E
░	L	░	N	░
V	E	S	T	░

6
S	P	E	A	K
░	E	░	M	░
G	R	O	A	N
░	C	░	Z	░
S	H	E	E	P

7
W	A	S	H	░
I	░	W	░	E
F	I	E	L	D
E	░	E	░	I
░	S	P	O	T

8
S	H	A	P	E
T	░	L	░	A
A	T	L	A	S
R	░	O	░	E
T	O	W	E	L

9
░	R	░	R	░
V	I	T	A	L
░	D	A	D	░
G	E	N	I	E
░	R	░	O	░

10
░	P	I	C	K
░	I	░	R	░
J	A	P	A	N
░	N	░	Z	░
C	O	P	Y	░

11
T	A	B	B	Y
░	L	░	E	░
L	O	Y	A	L
░	N	░	R	░
R	E	A	D	Y

Answers

Across

Thin biscuit (5)
A resident of Tel Aviv (7)
Book containing a story (5)
Young bird (5)
Marry someone (3)
1 These crash onto a beach (5)
3 Respond (5)
5 Fleshy edge of the mouth (3)
8 Thick slice of meat (5)
9 Incorrect (5)
0 Large, edible seafish with five pairs of limbs (7)
1 Green or purple fruit that grows on vines (5)

Down

1 Those with this condition often need an inhaler (6)
2 Type of school bag (7)
3 The coldest season of the year (6)
4 V, to a Roman (4)
5 Small loaf of bread (4)
10 Person who treats teeth (7)
12 Just one (6)
14 Ruler (6)
16 Short, thin tree branch (4)
17 Ancient Roman garment (4)

Puzzle 153

ACE PUZZLERS

Across

1 The elected people who run the country (11)
6 Tooth covering (6)
7 Swelling (4)
8 Neck warmer (5)
11 Think the same as someone else (5)
12 Happy expression (5)
13 Educational group (5)
17 Jumping insect that attaches itself to dogs and cats (4)
18 Earnings (6)
19 Extremely good; out of the ordinary (11)

Down

1 Journalists, as in "the ___" (5)
2 Woolly animal, similar to a small camel without a hump (5)
3 Not in operation (4)
4 Against the law (7)
5 You use these to count (7)
9 Difficult; complicated (7)
10 Let go of something (7)
14 Nut often gathered by squirrels (5)
15 Use your nose (5)
16 Tartan skirt (4)

Puzzle 152

ACE PUZZLERS

Across

7 Really terrible (5)
8 Unpleasant sound (5)
9 Biblical letter (7)
10 That girl; her (3)
11 Mix together smoothly (5)
13 This date (5)
15 Slippery with frozen water (3)
17 Picture made by sticking together scraps of paper (7)
20 Someone who protects a place (5)
21 Group of singers (5)

Down

1 Step (4)
2 Work building (6)
3 Apartment (4)
4 Use a needle to give medicine (6)
5 Fail to hit (4)
6 Long-stemmed crunchy green vegetable, often eaten raw (6)
11 River crossing (6)
12 A period of ten years (6)
14 Fire-breathing beast (6)
16 Casual word of agreement (4)
18 Shoe fastener (4)
19 A type of black tea, ___ Grey (4)

Puzzle 151

ACE PUZZLERS

Across

1 Vehicle for carrying injured people to hospital (9)

8 More than enough; also an anagram of "maple" (5)

9 Walk like a soldier (5)

10 Dickens's Dodger? (6)

12 Cause damage (4)

14 Become in need of rest (4)

15 Prickly plant that grows in hot countries (6)

17 Rope for walking a dog (5)

18 Large country house with surrounding grounds (5)

20 Mark left by a step (9)

Down

2 A chart which shows you where to go (3)

3 Handy (6)

4 Military force (4)

5 Dried grape (7)

6 Very large spider (9)

7 Science subject (9)

11 Violent windstorm (7)

13 Tool for putting in nails (6)

16 Online conversation (4)

19 Religious woman who lives in a convent (3)

Puzzle 150

Across

1 Close, but not completely exact (11)

7 Open a document on a computer (4)

8 Regard someone with respect (6)

9 Long seat for multiple people (5)

10 Sugary sweet (5)

13 Learn about something (5)

15 Someone who comes to visit (5)

17 Where polar bears live (6)

18 Famous science-fiction series, "Star ___" (4)

19 What flows in wires to power TVs and other devices (11)

Down

2 Stick out (7)

3 Cheaper in price (7)

4 December 25th, for short (4)

5 Someone from another planet (5)

6 A person who is against you (5)

11 Living in water (7)

12 Pudding (7)

13 Black playing card (5)

14 Parent's brother (5)

16 "The Lion King" villain (4)

Puzzle 149

ACE PUZZLERS

Across

3 "Up" on most maps (5)
6 Food energy unit (7)
7 Do very well at something (5)
8 Cheery; contented (5)
9 Winter illness (3)
11 Conjuring tricks (5)
13 Get pleasure from (5)
15 The opposite to a shake of the head (3)
18 Put words on paper (5)
19 House made of ice (5)
20 Strange; rare (7)
21 Chief town dignitary (5)

Down

1 A monkey's favourite fruit? (6)
2 Small toothed whale that appears to have a permanent smile (7)
3 Metal spike used for sewing (6)
4 Sprint contest (4)
5 Entrance lobby in a house (4)
10 Take your clothes off (7)
12 Red, blue or green, for example (6)
14 Criminal; fugitive (6)
16 Movie (4)
17 Theatre show (4)

ACE PUZZLERS

Puzzle 148

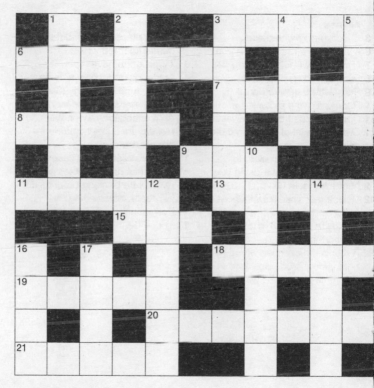

Across

Children play with these (4)

If you have a rash on your skin it may do this (4)

Female bird (3)

Party where people dance (5)

0 Record moving pictures (5)

1 Compass point opposite west (4)

2 Carved model of a person or animal (6)

4 Patterned Scottish cloth (6)

6 Travel through water using your hands and feet (4)

9 Device that's like a TV without pictures (5)

0 Opposite of goodbye (5)

1 Understand, as in "I ___" (3)

2 A relaxation exercise where you hold various body positions (4)

3 Labyrinth (4)

Down

2 Green place in the middle of a desert (5)

3 TV programme (4)

4 Ask someone to come to an event, such as a party (6)

5 Young army or police trainee (5)

6 An exciting journey or event (9)

8 Holiday for a newly married couple (9)

13 Crispy Indian pastry case filled with meat or vegetables (6)

15 Event with bucking broncos and bareback horse riding (5)

17 Formal ballroom dance (5)

18 Those people (4)